# Stress Warrior

Double Your Energy, Productivity and Focus
While You Drop Weight, Blood Sugar, Pain
and Anxiety by Recovering from Leaky Gut,
Oxidative Stress, and Adrenal Fatigue

*Dear Anne,
You are a Stress Warrior!
:)
Doni*

By Dr. Doni Wilson

ISBN 13: 978-1726690645

# Note from Dr Doni

If you are as busy as I think you are, right now you are looking for help to feel better faster so you can accomplish more each day. You may even be so busy, you don't have time to read this book. So I'm going to make it really easy for you. I can give you everything you want, and I am one phone call or an email message away. Email my office (office@doctordoni.com) and here is what will happen - we will set you up with a "done for you" health program.

I want to give you all your time back and do everything for you. You've probably been to a whole bunch of other doctors, bought a bunch of stuff, but you don't feel any better and you wonder what is wrong with you. It's actually not you. It's the system, and most practitioners don't have the right protocols. That's never gonna happen again. I'm an experienced doctor with over 18 years of experience who has worked with thousands of patients helping them to get back to feeling themselves, with energy, good sleep, stamina, focus, and the ability to get things done.

You want someone to run all your tests, interpret them, figure out exactly what to do and then tell you what to do in 15 minutes or less so that you feel 20 years younger in just a few weeks. That's exactly what I do.

**Here is what my program looks like:**

- High-Performer Evaluation: You'll be given my highest-level testing that is only available to executives, elite athletes and high-performers that detects how stress has affected your body and health. What this means for you are challenges that other doctors miss will be found so we can address them!

- Personalized Strategy: You'll get perfect clarity on what is needed to bring your hormones, neurotransmitters, digestion and immune system back on track.

- Elite Customized Supplements and Optimization Protocols: You'll receive a detailed step by step plan, supplement dosing and a printable chart with dosing instructions so that you can implement effortlessly

- Regular reminders so that you can...stay on track, get answers to questions, have access to guidance from me, do what is needed to keep moving forward

- Monthly Check-In and Maintenance: I'm committed to your highest results so that you have more impact, earn more income and experience the lifestyle you really want... (you have access to me to keep you on track and amplify your health and results)

- Access to my contacts of practitioners, specialists, resources and connections - the reason you need this is to optimize your recovery with the right team

- Access to my library of books, articles and master-classes and what this means for you is...you can continue learning as you go

- Menus, recipes and email tips - even when you have no time, you'll be operating at your highest level of energy, mood and memory

- Facebook Group - meet and network with other high-performers, executives and other stress warriors who share their wins, tools, resources, ideas and systems.

## This "Done for You" Stress Warrior Program is For You if You...

- Want to know EXACTLY how to optimize your energy, mood and sleep by unlocking your genetic potential

- Gain complete and total CLARITY on what to do with your health, fitness, food, diet, sleep and stress management

- How to do it so that you can be healthy even when stressed

- Want to look and feel 20 years younger so that you can get more done in less time and feel great while you do it...

- Increase your productivity and keep your edge as a high-performer

- Balance hormones and increase your motivation, intimacy and quality of the relationship with your spouse or partner

- Improve (or regain) your sex drive

- Wake up with 20%-100% more energy in the morning

- Become a champion sleeper - better and longer rest with more recovery

- Lower your stress and anxiety levels

- Amplify your concentration and focus effortlessly

- Extend your life by preventing dementia, diabetes and heart disease

- And you're willing to be compliant and committed to increasing and improving your health with less work, less stress with a dedicated doctor who has helped thousands of professionals and leaders who want to excel at what they do

**So that you can feel your best, be more productive at work or your business, and have more time to enjoy the people and things you love.**

Reach out to my office and we can get started, whether you read this book or not: office@doctordoni.com.

# Table of Contents

# Introduction

This book is about you. You are an elite performer. You're probably an executive, CEO, entrepreneur, artist, performer, parent (or hoping to be a parent), lawyer, practitioner, and/or leader in your community.

You value time and time compression more than anything. Imagine what it would feel like to get a day or two back every single week. What would you do with that extra day? That's what this book is all about. The number one thing that is preventing you from having everything you want is stress. I developed a program to get your time and health back. I call it the Stress Warrior Program.

## What is a Stress Warrior?

A person who is juggling priorities all day (and night) long while recovering from stress such as from building a business, a relationship, a loss and grief, fertility/miscarriage, infection (HPV, Lyme, EBV), toxicity (mold, chemicals), travel and/or being a caretaker to a parent and/or pet.

Essentially a Stress Warrior is faced with doing the near impossible most every day. Th ere is no chance of not having stress. Instead, a Stress Warrior is forced to learn to deal with stress. The challenge is: how to be healthy while stressed.

A (single) parent, entrepreneur, executive or CEO who is juggling priorities all day (and night) long while recovering from stress such as from a relationship, a loss and grief, fertility/miscarriage, infection (HPV, Lyme, EBV), toxicity (mold, chemicals), travel and/or being a caretaker to a parent and/or pet.

Every minute and hour of each day stress in various forms decreases your energy, sleep, productivity, and memory, and in the process, you are less able to keep up and the stress piles higher. It doesn't work to delay stress recovery to a weekend retreat or vacation, because inevitably more stress shows up.

In fact, a Stress Warrior often feels that stress follows them. It fills in any extra space and for good reason – Stress Warriors tend to be good at handling stress. This is often because Stress Warriors actually have genetic tendencies that help them respond to stressful situations. They are drawn to stress and are often a leader when it comes to dealing with stress. They become experts at stress.

And yet still, stress affects their health. Even though as humans we are built to be stress responding and recovering beings, depending the extent of stress exposure and our genetic predispositions, eventually stress takes a toll on our bodies and minds.

The part we need help with is the recovery from stress so that stress doesn't take us out of commission. This is where self-care comes in, which can be a foreign concept to a Stress Warrior who is used to taking care of others before herself/himself.

When a Stress Warrior learns to integrate self-care into her/his busy schedule, that is when she/he has the power to shield herself from the effects of stress and keep doing what she loves.

## What health challenges does a Stress Warrior face?

Fatigue

Fertility issues

Recurrent Infections

Insomnia

Anxiety

Depression

Migraines

Allergies

Digestive issues

Decreased memory or even dementia

Skin rashes

Pain

Autoimmunity

Menstrual irregularities – heavy, painful periods and/or PMS symptoms

Peri-menopausal symptoms – hot flashes, night sweats, joint pain, weight gain, and headaches

## Here's the thing: it is possible to feel better.

I know because I have been there. I too am a Stress Warrior. I've been attracted to stress my whole life. That could be due to my genetics and/or my early childhood exposure to stress. I learned to accept and thrive under stressful situations, which lead me to choose more stress. I finished two Bachelor's degrees in four years, and then completed naturopathic medical school while training to be a midwife (which involved many sleepless nights).

Then I moved across the country to New York right after 911 and started my practice as a naturopathic doctor in a state that doesn't license the profession, so I learned to run a legislative effort and non-profit organization, which I did for over ten years while raising my daughter (who was born at home) and choosing to divorce my husband.

I started my own business and practice, bought my own house, and self-published my first book (The Stress Remedy) by the time I was 40 years old. And then, after years of helping thousands of patients, as well as pursuing self-development, (including a type of therapy called EMDR which is known to help with stress recovery and training in mindfulness,) to help me recover from stressful experiences, I realized that I was not implementing enough self-care in my life and in my love relationship of 12 years. I started making more choices to take care of me, my needs and my goals, and that lead me to write this book – The Stress Warrior.

The gift of being a Stress Warrior is that I see each day and experience as an opportunity to learn and grow. And that is what helped me recover from relationship loss, years of migraines involving days of vomiting, menstrual pain, pregnancy loss, allergies, anxiety, depression and fatigue. It is by thinking of myself as a Stress Warrior that I face the day and how I hope to inspire you as well.

## I know I'm not alone.

I've been helping women, men and children recover from stress for over 18 years. I know there are CEOs, teachers, athletes, college students, care-takers, artists, lawyers, judges, parents, and practitioners out there who are struggling to keep up with stress. I know because I have met them and supported them in their process of stress recovery and resilience.

They experience fatigue from lack of sleep, anxiety from too much pressure, weight gain, hormone imbalances, blood sugar issues, food cravings, eating disorders, skin rashes, digestive troubles, pregnancy loss, and mood fluctuations all because their bodies are trying to tell them that the stress is too much. But how to get off the treadmill? If we stop the money doesn't come in, things don't get done, and still the stress increases. And so, we find a way to continue, often by choosing things that can also add more stress such as sugar, alcohol, sleeping pills, pain meds, anti-depressants, immune-suppressants and antibiotics.

More and more people are seeing the vicious cycle and wanting to find a way out of it. I hear you. There has to be a way. There is a way.

I've learned from my experience with stress and created a path to help you stop the cycle and reverse engineer health.

It turns out that I love to read studies. I love to understand the human body and how it responds to stress. I've read the books on stress, the studies on what reduces stress, and the research on how stress causes major health issues such as autoimmunity, Alzheimer's, diabetes, cancer, and heart disease. I've figured out how we can identify exactly the way stress is affecting your body, and how to reverse it using diet changes, nutrients, herbs and a few other approaches that don't add to the stress.

I've tried it all out on myself to see what works. I delved into the genetics of stress as well, and figured out which gene SNPs are involved in how we respond to stress and which gene SNPs require that we implement more stress recovery. I've put it all together for you in a step by step approach that you can do on your own at home, with the help of a group of Stress Warriors, or by working one-on-one with me (or a practitioner I have trained).

The main thing I want you to know is that it is possible to feel better, and without bringing everything to a halt. Now in the process you may realize some things in your life are no longer working for you – a job, a relationship, a home, a schedule. You may realize big changes you want and need to make in order to reach your main goal – health and wellness to enjoy the people and places you love for as long as you can.

No matter what, you'll still have exposure to some sort of stress, whether emotional, physical (injuries or infections), toxins (in our air, food, water), or life circumstances that we can't control. And that is why learning to be a Stress Warrior who is resilient to stress by implementing self-care is so important.

## In this book, I'll guide you to learn:

What is stress

What is the stress response

How stress affects us

How stress affects you

What is leaky gut

What is dysbiosis and the microbiome

What is oxidative stress

What is adrenal distress

How to integrate self CARE

How to implement my three-step protocol: Remove, Restore, Resilience

In the book, my goal is to explain the science and how our bodies work in a way that helps you be successful with your health. I often joke – if only our bodies came with an instruction manual! Well here it is; at least what I find to be the most important information for my high-performing patients.

Along the way, in each chapter, I share "take away notes" and essential steps you can implement right away. I also share interviews with patients I consider to be Stress Warriors because I think you'll relate and learn from their experiences. Then I put it all together in my Self CARE Protocol for you to follow as you recover from stress and become a resilient Stress Warrior.

At the end of this book, you will also find information about resources to support you on your Stress Warrior journey, including online programs, consultation packages and health panels, as well as products, herbs and supplements I recommend.

It's not about being perfect. Just the opposite. It is about being and doing your best at any point in time, and being aware and open to learn from the experience. Forgiveness, self-love, and support for you and your body is the way of a Stress Warrior.

By implementing these ways of being with yourself, with others, and with the world, you'll be about to double your energy, focus and productivity so you can get out there, accomplish your goals and make your dreams come true while feeling good and living a long, healthy life.

I can't wait to tell you more!

# Section 1

## Understanding Stress

# CHAPTER 1

# Stress and the Stress Response

### What is Stress

**W**e so often hear the word "stress," that we dismiss it.

We even hear it at the doctor's office – as in, your condition is caused by stress. But then what? What caused the stress and what can we do about it? Unless we resolve ourselves to always feeling unwell and continually adding more medications to the list in order to combat the effects of stress, the only alternative is to face our stress and find ways to recover from it.

First let's get to know the stresses around us. There are some stresses we can't predict or do anything about. There are other stresses that are essentially a part of life. And still others that come into play when we challenge ourselves and have a desire to learn and grow. There are still other stresses that are part of our day to day reality.

Let me be clear. The goal is NOT to avoid all stress. Nor is it to be "stress-free."

It doesn't make sense to replace one illusion (of being invincible to stress) with another (being completely free of stress). I'm not here to give you some impossible goal or illogical plan.

I'm here to say that there are ways for us to choose our stresses carefully and to recover from those stresses we do not choose.

Think back to Maslow's theory of human needs. Shelter, clothing, food. And the lack of those things is a stress. So, at the most fundamental level, stress is the lack of having our needs met.

According to stress psychology, major stresses include death of a loved one, divorce, moving homes, abuse, crisis, trauma. Those are absolutely stresses. We know from studies that when people, both adults and children, are exposed to these major stresses, it has a major impact on health. And not just mental health, as one might suspect, but physical health as well.

Then there are all of the day-to-day stresses that we tend to take for granted because they are not major stresses. Things like deadlines at work, financial stresses, stresses in relationships and communications, being a parent, owning a business, traveling between time zones, not getting enough sleep, and being overstimulated by technology and light exposure.

Add to that anything that requires that our bodies respond in order to protect us. This includes toxins in our environment (food, air and water) that we inhale or ingest and that affect our bodies and health in some way. Certain foods and beverages act as a stress by changing our blood sugar levels, triggering an immune response, and/or requiring that our liver work harder to detoxify them.

When you get down to it, stress is all around us. It becomes absolutely clear that it would be impossible to avoid stress. Quite the opposite. Stress is part of life. And we as humans are built to respond to stress.

## What is the Stress Response

After years of studying science and human health, I came to realization that everything about our bodies is intended to help us respond and adapt to stress.

Our brain is a stress radar system. It notices and responds to any change, sound, movement, stimulation, sending a signal through what is referred to as the Hypothalamic-Pituitary-Adrenal axis (HPA axis) and the sympathetic nervous system.

The sympathetic nervous system makes adrenaline, what we think of as the fight or flight response. Adrenaline speeds our heart rate and our thinking, and gets us ready to run or react to the stress at hand.

The HPA axis tells the adrenal glands to make more adrenaline as well as cortisol, our main stress hormone.

Cortisol then signals out to the rest of the body to respond to the stress instead of continuing usual activities, like digestion.

You see, cortisol and adrenaline are around all the time, not just when we are stressed. Cortisol is the only hormones that is naturally higher in the morning, when we wake, and gradually decreases to its lowest point in the evening, when we go to sleep. Adrenaline remains at a steady level throughout the day and night.

It is when we are exposed to stress that cortisol and adrenaline shift from their natural state to help us respond to the stress. And with a healthy stress response, the levels return to optimal when the stress is gone.

We need stress and a stress response in order to be healthy and for our bodies to do what we need them to do. For example, when a woman is in labor (as in childbirth), a certain amount of cortisol and adrenaline is needed in order for labor to progress naturally. With either too much or not enough stress and stress hormones, labors slows, and interventions become necessary.

When we are exposed to too much stress for too long, which is unique to each individual, that is when cortisol and adrenaline have a difficult time coming back to optimal. Our bodies adapt to the stress in our environment, and can get stuck in stress mode, or become depleted by stress. I refer to this as Adrenal Distress.

As we are exposed to various stresses, as part of life, our bodies attempt to adapt and recover from stress. Our bodies are literally in a constant state of either reacting to, or recovering from, stress. Even babies and children are in a perpetual state of reacting to, and recovering from, stress.

As we respond to stress, it turns on our genetic tendencies. Stress literally changes our genes and shortens our protection from stress. This is measured by something called telomeres. Telomeres are the section of genetic information at the end of each strand of DNA. The length of your telomeres is used as a way to assess your age. The longer your telomeres, the younger and more resilient you are compared to others in your same age group.

In this way, stress and your ability to recover from it effectively determines your youthfulness and the length of your life. In fact, when the stress is too great for our body at any point in time, that is when life ends. That's how important it is to make choices and become a master at responding and recovering from stress.

## TAKE AWAY NOTES:

Stress includes emotional stress as well as: _____

_____

Cortisol levels should be _____early in the day and

_____later in the day.

A telomere indicates _____

# CHAPTER 2

# How Stress Affects Us

**E**ven though the thought of how stress affects us can be quite scary – adding yet more stress – for a Stress Warrior, the only option is to face it head on and learn what it takes to be healthy while stressed. The first step in that process is to understand stress. By understanding the trouble it causes, we can then break those patterns and make choices to reverse it.

Let me give you a sense of what happens in our bodies when we are stressed:

Cortisol and adrenaline increase.

Digestion decreases, which means food is not digested well.

Nutrients used to rebuild intestinal cells are used to help respond to the stress.

Thyroid hormone production decreases.

Ovarian and testicular hormone production decreases.

Blood sugar levels fluctuate or increase.

Oxidative stress level increases.

Inflammation increases.

Neurotransmitters are produced and used up more quickly.

The immune system is less able to protect from infections while responding to stress.

All of this leads us to feel tired, irritable, anxious, bloated, not sleeping well, decreased memory, weight gain (or loss for some), and less and less ambition to do what we love.

That is the quick overview of how stress affects us. Now let's dive into exactly how all that happens.

## Repercussions of the Stress Response

Let's pick up from where we left off with the stress response in chapter 1. When we experience stress, in any form, cortisol spikes, and then returns to "normal" for that time of day.

When cortisol spikes, it sends messages to turn off or decrease function in our digestion, immune system, and other hormones. It also increases adrenaline and shifts neurotransmitter levels. This all allows us to respond to the stress in the moment.

The issue is that in our modern, daily lives, we are exposed to stress (in various forms) left and right, from one minute to the next. We hardly ever have a chance to allow our bodies to come out of the stress response.

Some of us have gene SNPs (single nucleotide polymorphism) or variations on MTHFR, COMT and/or MAO, which are known as **warrior genes** because they help us react and respond to stress. Those of us with these gene SNPs are more susceptible to the effects of stress and require even more stress recovery.

## Four Main Systems Affected by Stress

When we are stressed all the time, our **digestion, immune system, hormones and nervous system** don't get much of a chance to do their thing.

That's why we tend to develop digestive issues (ulcers, stomachaches and IBS), more infections (colds, bladder infections, herpes outbreaks, etc), skipped periods and decreased fertility (decreased ovulation), low thyroid function, and elevated blood sugar (insulin not working well) which leads to weight gain.

We also tend to have decreased neurotransmitters, such as low serotonin (mostly made in the gut and depleted by stress), low GABA (leading to more anxiety and sleep issues), and either high or low adrenaline, which disrupts our mood, sleep, memory and focus.

Let's have a closer look at each of the four systems and how they are affected by stress.

# Digestion

Stress essentially turns off our digestion, in order for us to deal with the stress at hand. When stressed, we don't digest food well, the cells lining our intestines are damaged and don't repair as well, nutrients are not absorbed, and our healthy gut bacteria (microbiome) decrease as well.

All of these effects of stress lead to and perpetuate an issue called Leaky Gut (or intestinal permeability). The leaking that occurs with leaky gut is through the walls of the intestines to the inside of our bodies.

You see, the intestinal walls are made up of tiny cells, all lined up next to each other and held together by proteins. In a healthy digestion, our food is digested and the nutrients traverse through and between these healthy cells to get into our bodies. Meanwhile undigested food, bacteria, and toxic substances are not allowed to cross over. Normally these intestinal cells are replaced every few days.

With stress, the intestinal cells are depleted, damaged and not replaced effectively. The cells are then not able to do their job to prevent undigested food and bacteria from leaking across. When food leaks through undigested, our immune system (which is sitting on the other side of the intestinal cells) reacts in an effort to protect us. This causes food allergies and food sensitivities. Several different types of antibodies and immune messengers (cytokines) respond.

This leads to inflammatory signals locally and throughout your body causing such symptoms as rashes, headaches, pain and anxiety (anxiety is inflammation in the nervous system). This inflammation makes you more susceptible to infections, autoimmunity and weight gain.

The inflammation stemming from leaky gut lasts for days and even weeks. It can be subtle, building up over time, such that it would be hard for you to connect a certain food or reaction to the symptoms. All you know is that you feel worse and worse over time. This is when a food sensitivity panel can be very useful for showing us which foods are triggering inflammation (and therefore which foods to avoid) and demonstrating the presence of leaky gut.

Stress and cortisol also disrupt the healthy bacteria in our intestines. We end up with less of the good bacteria and are more likely to have overgrowing bacteria and/or yeast. Overgrowing and pathogenic bacteria product toxins which cause yet more inflammation and intestinal permeability, further perpetuating the effects of leaky gut and stress throughout your body.

Specialized stool panels are able to identify bacteria based on their DNA, showing us exactly what has gotten out of balance and which bacteria need more support.

## Hormones

Stress and cortisol also disrupts our hormone levels. You name it, every hormone is disrupted by stress.

13

One of the most common to be thrown off track is the thyroid hormone. Many people have the symptoms of low thyroid function, such as fatigue, weight gain, and low mood, whether or not blood work actually shows decreased thyroid function. This can be related to cortisol, because elevated cortisol suppresses thyroid function. It can also be due to oxidative stress (we'll discuss more soon) in the mitochondria, whose job it is to activate thyroid hormone.

Low thyroid function is also often caused when the immune system mistakenly attacks the thyroid as part of an autoimmune issue called Hashimoto's, which is caused by stress and leaky gut. More about the immune system in a minute.

Elevated cortisol also makes it harder to keep your blood sugar on track. That is because it decreases the ability of insulin to move glucose into your cells. When insulin is not able to move glucose out of your blood, that leaves you with high blood sugar, which is associated with metabolic syndrome and diabetes.

Stress and cortisol also makes it more likely that your menstrual cycle will be irregular or that you will have PMS, fertility issues and/or peri-menopausal symptoms. That is because cortisol turns off the ovaries. Ovulation doesn't happen, leaving you with low estrogen and/or progesterone, and less ability to ovulate and conceive. Doctors will tell you the only option is to take a birth control pill to regulate your cycle, or fertility medications that cause you to ovulate, but that is not addressing the real issue.

14

Stress in various forms is the underlying cause. Address it, and hormones come back to balance.

## Immune System

We become more susceptible to infections (colds, viruses, bacterial and yeast infections), and we also become more likely to have allergies and autoimmunity. The effect of stress on your immune system is influenced by your genetic tendencies.

It's not often all of those things at once. You might first notice more frequent colds or other infections such as herpes, HPV, EBV/mono, and Lyme. For others, it may be worsening allergies, eczema, or histamine issues (mast cell activation syndrome).

It's common to get through infections and allergies with antibiotics and steroidal medications. In the moment, they are often needed. But if needed over and over, leaky gut develops, healthy gut bacteria are disrupted, and autoimmunity is triggered.

Autoimmunity is when the immune system gets confused and starts to attack your own healthy cells. It mistakes your healthy cells for something foreign. This immune confusion is known to be triggered by stress, intestinal permeability (leaky gut) and disrupted gut bacteria. By this point, external stress has created internal stress. And the standard medical solution involves yet still more immune suppression.

15

Instead, I encourage you to become aware of this pattern and do whatever you can to turn it around.

It's possible to support a healthy immune response to infections, avoid the need for antibiotics and steroids (whenever possible), decrease allergic responses, and reverse autoimmunity.

I say this with confidence because I've helped people do this for the past 20 years, and I've done it for my own health.

Autoimmunity is in my genes, and yet I don't have autoimmunity. I have had severe allergies and frequent infections, but no longer do. I've taken antibiotics only once in my life. I want this for you. Start by recovering from stress. Get your cortisol back on track. Heal leaky gut. Optimize gut bacteria. You can do this.

## Nervous System

Neurotransmitters like serotonin, dopamine, adrenaline, and GABA are all negatively affected by stress. When we are stressed, cortisol levels shift and our stress genes turn up or down the volume on processing neurotransmitters.

Because we don't digest food well when stressed, and because leaky gut happens, our nutrients and neurotransmitters (many of which are made in our intestines) get depleted. Our bacteria become imbalanced and send inflammatory signals to the nervous system through what is called the "gut-brain axis."

16

No wonder we are more likely to experience anxiety, depression and decreased memory and focus when we are stressed. When calming neurotransmitters like serotonin and GABA are too low, we are likely to feel anxious, overwhelmed and not sleep well. Our buffer to stress becomes depleted. When stimulating neurotransmitters, like dopamine and adrenaline, are depleted, we are likely to feel tired and brain fog.

It's absolutely possible to take steps to recover from stress. Neurotransmitters are made in our bodies out of amino acids from the protein in our food. When neurotransmitter levels are low - due to stress - we can use amino acids to rebalance neurotransmitter levels.

We can measure neurotransmitters in urine. This way we know exactly what's too low or too high. Then we use the precursor amino acids, in dosing specific to you and in a particular order. I've been doing this for over 15 years, so I've seen every pattern and have created a protocol to guide you.

Just know - it's possible to rebuild your resilience to stress. Your body knows how. It just needs the right ingredients. I'm going to be teaching you how to rebalance each of these systems – digestion, hormones, immune system and nervous system – in this book.

## The Vicious Cycle of Stress

Basically, stress throws off our normal cortisol pattern and that throws off the rest of our hormones, digestion, nervous system and immune function. This all leads to inflammation, intestinal permeability (known as leaky gut), oxidative stress, and adrenal distress. We will be covering each of those areas in more detail in upcoming chapters.

What I want you to know is that the effects of stress are reversible.

This is why knowing and optimizing your cortisol and adrenaline levels is SOOOOO important! The levels could be too high or too low, and at different times of day. Cortisol can be measured in urine or saliva (or blood) four times in a day so we can know exactly what your cortisol is up to. Adrenaline can be measured in urine.

And once we know your levels, we can give the right support with herbs and nutrients to correct them. Then once we get your cortisol back on track, all you have to do is keep it that way using self-care (more on that to come).

The more we know and understand about the effects of stress, the better we can address each of those issues and reverse the effects of stress. Then, and in the process, we become such masters of stress and what our bodies need in order to stay healthy while stressed, that we achieve resilience to stress. Essentially, we become Stress Warriors.

Make sense?  : )

------------------------------------------------

## TAKE AWAY NOTES:

Stress disrupts these 4 systems:

1. _____

2. _____

3. _____

4. _____

Leaky gut, which is caused by stress, means that the

_____lining the intestines

are _____and allowing _____ and _____to leak
through to trigger the immune system.

This leads to _____ throughout the body.

It is possible to measure _____ and

_____ to know how stress has affected me.

------------------------------------------------

19

# CHAPTER 3

# Stress, Genetics, Methylation and Oxidative Stress

Genetics don't determine our health. Stress exposure does.

That's because our genetic tendencies are turned on by stress. This is referred to as epigenetics.

I'm not referring to congenital conditions in which a person is born with a major genetic defect. Even then, many genetic conditions are improved with diet, nutrient and lifestyle changes.

I'm referring to your unique genetic and familial predispositions to heart disease, diabetes, allergies, autoimmunity, Alzheimer's, and the list goes on. We are talking about the health issues that develop through life.

For a long time, it was thought that we could *not* do anything about our genetic predispositions. That our genes had a major influence that we could not override. In fact, many people would give up on making healthy choices because they were led to believe that it wouldn't make a difference.

Research has now discovered that our genes are actually only 5% to 15% of what determines our health; the other 75% to 95% is all about diet, exercise, stress, toxins, and sleep.

That means **your health is not set in stone – don't feel resigned to your genetic predispositions.** We can now look at your genes and use that information to give your body what it needs and improve your health.

The U.S. Centers for Disease Control and Prevention (CDC) has identified that *all* of the major chronic health issues that lead to medical costs and death can be prevented by addressing diet and lifestyle. It is in only very few cases, such as with Down's syndrome or cystic fibrosis, that single gene mutations influence health in a major way. However, most chronic health conditions such as diabetes and obesity are less determined by your genes than by what you do to support your health on a daily basis.

**Think of it this way:** If your genes are the recipe, your food, sleep, exercise, toxin exposure, and stress are the ingredients, and your health is the dish you make – each time you make the recipe, the dish may turn out slightly different. If you add a little more or less salt for example, or if you add the ingredients to the bowl in a slightly different order, or if the cook time varies, the dish may taste very different.

While the recipe stays the same, the outcome can still vary. Just as the dish can be improved with variations in the ingredients, you can greatly influence your health with the foods you choose and the amount of sleep, stress, toxic exposure, and exercise you get. And the choices you make each day can influence how the "recipe" turns out.

"Our genes are our genes and that is not going to change... but how they influence our health *can* change."

Instead of using your genetics to predict what will go wrong, **by knowing your personal genetic make-up, we can work out what individual adjustments you need to make in order to support your body**.

Say for example you have a gene variation that decreases your ability to metabolize or "detoxify" alcohol. For you, avoiding alcohol will be beneficial for your health. Or say you're like me and have a SNP (single nucleotide polymorphism) that means your body struggles to turn folic acid into folate – known as an MTHFR MUTATION – then your health will improve if you avoid products that contain the synthetic nutrient folic acid, and may improve if you take folate (5-methylfolate) instead.

This is why I now recommend that my patients do a genetic so we can tailor their treatment to their specific genetic pattern. Essentially it has to do with stress recovery. The more you support your body under stress, the less susceptible you'll be to genetic predispositions.

A lot of the influence stresses have on our health comes down to somethings called methylation and oxidative stress.

## First Let's Discuss Methylation

Methylation is how our bodies use B vitamins for good things like making healthy new cells, protecting our DNA and processing neurotransmitters. Without healthy methylation, we become susceptible to the negative effects of stress. Taking the right amount of B vitamins for your body will help protect you from stress.

However, it is important to know that if your body is currently overwhelmed by stress, then you will not be able to use B vitamins effectively, methylation will get stuck, and in that situation, B vitamins could even make you feel worse. This is especially the case if you have genetic SNPs like MTHFR, MTRR, COMT, MAO, and others.

That's why the BEST first step is to address your stress, no matter your genetic predispositions. As you reverse the effects of stress, you'll also be able to reverse and prevent health issues even if in your genes. By knowing your gene SNPs, you'll have even more power to know what your body needs.

And by optimizing methylation, you'll be supporting the production of anti-oxidants, which protect us from oxidative stress.

# Oxidative Stress

Oxidative stress in the human body, like rust on a car, results in signs that we normally associate with aging—grey hair, wrinkles, memory loss, and fatigue.

Like rust, oxidative stress occurs in our bodies when our cells and tissue is oxidized. It is confusing to think that oxygen, which is essential for life, is also damaging to our lives when it overwhelms our body's ability to recycle it and recover from what are referred to as free radicals—oxygen molecules that have the potential to cause us damage.

Oxidative stress is not, however, simply a natural result of getting older that we just have to accept. It is the result of:

- Emotional stress and elevated cortisol levels;
- Toxic exposure, including to metals like mercury and lead, as well as pollutants, smoke, and exhaust fumes;
- Elevated blood sugar levels;
- Not enough anti-oxidants like vitamin C, selenium, and zinc in our diets;
- Physical stress, like intense workouts and/or injuries.

When oxidative stress occurs, it is harder for your body to bounce back from stress.

Injuries heal more slowly, infections become more likely, and further disruption in the balance of hormones and immune function results.

That's simply because your cells won't be as healthy when oxidative stress is high, and the *mitochondria* that produce energy inside your cells won't be able to do their job well. So you are likely to feel tired, achy, worn out, and just not yourself. Refer to the Resources section for more information about mitochondria.

Once you understand that oxidative stress affects every cell in your body, it makes more sense that research finds it plays a role in all major health issues including diabetes, heart disease, cancer, asthma, degenerative diseases, and neurological diseases such as Alzheimer's and Parkinson's.

It is also associated with many common conditions in various areas of the body such as cataracts, arrhythmia (abnormal heart rhythms), anxiety, depression, chronic fatigue syndrome, fibromyalgia, BPH, kidney stones, macular degeneration, psoriasis, rheumatoid arthritis, GERD, hypertension, and tinnitus.

Basically, if you don't feel well or something isn't working as well as it used to, it's probably because of oxidative stress. It's part of being human, and it's the focus of all anti-aging efforts. The more we can use your genetic information to help you recover from stress, the more we can protect you from oxidative stress.

# Looking at the Whole Picture

It is important to keep in mind that, just as your genetics don't absolutely determine your health, SNPs (gene mutations) don't absolutely influence your health either. **We have to look at both your SNPs and some actual measures of your health status to determine how, and if, your genetics are influencing your health.**

Even someone who has an MTHFR mutation should have tests done to see how their body is currently functioning before adding folate to their daily routine.

By looking at your genetic panel, we get a sense of the potential "traffic jams" – pathways in your metabolism that make you YOU! You might be sensitive to caffeine, environmental toxins, or certain medications. Or perhaps your body needs more of a certain nutrient or anti-oxidant in order to keep up under stress.

Then we follow up by testing your actual nutrient levels, as well as hormones, neurotransmitters, and anti-oxidants so that we can find out whether your genes are currently influencing your health. If they are, then we can introduce diet changes, nutrients, herbs and other possible interventions to address that pathway.

**The health panels that can help us know where to support your body:**

- **Blood work** including, amongst others: CBC, metabolic panel, C-reactive protein (an indicator of inflammation), thyroid stimulating hormone (TSH), 25 OH vitamin D, and hemoglobin A1c (average blood sugar)

- **IgA and IgG food sensitivity panel** so we can find out whether foods you are eating are trigging inflammation, which then slows methylation and increases oxidative stress

- **Cortisol** (either salivary or dried urine) in four samples – morning, mid-day, evening, and bedtime

- **Neurotransmitters** (urine) – serotonin, dopamine, GABA, glutamate, norepinephrine and epinephrine, as well as the metabolites of these neurotransmitters

- **Organic acids** (urine) – metabolites that indicate levels of oxidative stress, mitochondrial function, glutathione (a major anti-oxidant) and nutrient status

- **Methylation panel** (blood) including homocysteine and methylmalonic acid to determine how well your body is using B vitamins to benefit your health

- **8-OHdG** that is measured in urine; elevated levels indicate high oxidative stress

- **Genetic panel** so we can get to know your SNPs and what may be needed to support your body

This information gives us a snapshot of where you are at this point in time based on your genetics and your food, sleep, toxic exposure, stress, and exercise. From there, we can take steps to address your specific requirements and prevent health issues from developing. In this way, your genes can unlock the truth of what your body needs.

## One More Factor to Consider – Bacteria

There is one other factor that plays a significant role in our health, and that is the genetics of the bacteria that live inside our bodies (in our intestines, for example). We are not just *us*; we are us *plus* the bacteria and other organisms that have an influence over how our genes are expressed and whether mutations end up affecting our daily lives and health. This is why it's important to not just think about how you can protect your body, but how you can protect your bacteria as well. (We'll cover this more in a later chapter)

These bacteria are influenced by the same factors that influence human genes: foods, stress, sleep, toxins, and exercise. They are also greatly influenced by antibiotics, so being able to *prevent* the need for antibiotics is one of the single best health prevention tactics you can implement.

I would add one more test to the list; **a stool analysis to evaluate the DNA of the bacteria in your gut.** There are several labs that offer this type of testing now. As I tell my patients every day, I believe this to be the future of medicine – research that will help us know how best to return the most optimal balance of bacteria to our digestive tracts.

To simplify this: I think of all these things that influence our genes, our gut bacteria and their genes, and therefore our overall health, as stress or potential stress.

Just as psycho-emotional stress affects our health, so does the stress of high-sugar foods and beverages, the stress of not getting adequate sleep, the stress of being exposed to toxins in our food, air, water, and personal care products, as well as the stress of not enough exercise. While you are born with your genes, you do have the ability to greatly influence how those genes affect your health by managing the bacteria and your exposure to various forms of stress.

## Applying the 4 Key Elements of Wellness

Since we know the stresses that negatively affect health, we can take steps to reduce our exposure to those stresses. And by doing that you'll also be preventing your genetic predispositions from affecting your health.

The four areas that influence both our human genes and the genes of the organisms living in our bodies are the four key elements of wellness: **Diet**; **exercise**; **stress**; and **sleep**.

That means that if your goal is to live as healthily as you can for as long as you can – which happens to be *my* health goal – then you'll want to make diet choices, exercise routines, stress reduction techniques, product choices, and sleep essentials all a part of your daily routine. Even if you don't know your genetic SNPs, these general steps can help.

I organize them into a plan we can implement called CARE: Clean eating, Adequate sleep, Reducing stress and Exercise. I'll be guiding you through implementing CARE later in this book.

Now, of course, we are all human – we will trip up sometimes. We will skip exercising or binge on junk food from time to time. But being overly vigilant or stressed out about the things that affect your health can actually outweigh all the good you are doing.

It's all about being committed to your goal while also being unattached or un-stressed about the outcome. That's not an easy thing to do, believe me – it takes practice, awareness, and a willingness to learn. It's not about perfection but instead – consistently prioritizing yourself, feeling connected with yourself, and being empowered to make choices that are in line with your vision.

The sooner you realize your exposure to stress and oxidative stress, start making choices that help you recover from it, the better chance you have of reversing the effects of stress and optimizing your health.

# CHAPTER 4

# Three Phases of Stress Recovery

**Y**ou see, we are all exposed to stress. Stress is a part of life. But ignoring and dismissing stress as impossible to control is not the solution. We need to learn to embrace stress. After all, we need stress in order to thrive and accomplish our goals. It is a matter of supporting ourselves and our bodies through stress in order to keep up with stress and to maintain our health.

It just so happens that I've been thinking of healing and wellness this way for quite a long time. I've studied it, tried it out on myself, and used it with thousands of patients for close to 20 years. Over that time, I developed a three-step system of implementing stress recovery, and I'm going to share it with you now.

## STEP 1: Remove the Stressors

"Stress" is not just a feeling or mental state; it's also a physical state. Your body becomes stressed when it cannot handle what is happening to it. Anything that puts your body in a state of stress is a "stressor."

Psychological stress, injury, infection, toxins, and trauma – all these kinds of stress will affect four main systems in our bodies: Digestion, immune system, nervous system, and hormones. When these systems become imbalanced, the can lead to three main health issues that can trap us in an ongoing state of poor health: Adrenal distress, intestinal permeability (leaky gut), and imbalanced metabolism (blood sugar issues). We will discuss these issues in more detail in upcoming chapters.

Every one of us is exposed to stress/stressors every day; it is impossible to eliminate them altogether. However, some stressors – such as toxins or allergens in our air, food or water, or infections in our body – can trigger inflammation and dysfunction in our bodies, making us feel unwell in some way.

Taking steps to address and avoid these toxins can make a significant difference and help your body to recover. The only way to start the healing process is to eliminate (or at least minimize) our exposure to the stressors that are triggering our symptoms. Without first removing these stressors from our environment, we'll just end up going in circles, experiencing the same problems over and over.

Of course, you won't necessarily know WHAT to remove, simply by looking at your symptoms. The only way to know for sure is to get checked for food sensitivities, oxidative stress, toxins, metals, and infections.

Whenever I start working with a new patient, the first thing I usually do is discuss which specialty panels are available to help us identify what is most likely triggering negative health symptoms. The next step is to create a plan for removing those triggers from their environment. Sometimes, this can require significant changes in the patient's diet and lifestyle. Also, if the exposure has been going on for a while, it may take some time for the effects of those changes to become noticeable.

If you have a current infection (a cold, bladder infection, or other active infection), it is also essential to take steps to address the infection as it can put stress on your immune system and your entire body. More chronic infections, such as Lyme, HPV and EBV, will improve as you address and recover from stress. The reason the chronic infections exists is because your immune system is depleted.

Most conventional medical doctors will prescribe antibiotics to address bacterial infections, and while in some situations they are necessary, they can compromise the digestive system and become a "stress" if used over and over. For that reason, my goal is to teach patients how to use natural approaches (herbs and nutrients) to get rid of infections whenever possible. As you recover from stress, your immune system will get better and better at fighting off infections.

At this point I encourage you to start to make a list of possible stressors affecting your health. Examples are:

Foods

Sugar

Alcohol

Pesticides (non-organic food)

Insecticides and other chemicals

Unfiltered water

Air from traffic or other toxic exposures

Mold exposure

Metals, such as amalgam dental fillings

Infections

Medications

Lack of sleep

Blood sugar fluctuations

Skipping meals

Large meals

Allergens

Stressful relationships

Not saying no

What steps can start to take to address or eliminate these stresses?

I included resources at the end of this book to help you identify products and services to help you decrease your stress exposure. You may find that your best solution is to work with a naturopathic doctor who can help you identify stresses and how to deal with them safely and effectively.

---

---

---

---

## STEP 2: Restore the Balance

To perform as it is meant to, ALL your bodily systems – hormones, metabolism, digestion, nervous, adrenal, and immune system – need to be in balance. Even methylation and oxidation needs to be in balance. The reason stressors trigger ill health is that they create imbalances in these systems.

And because all these systems are interconnected, if one system gets out of balance, it can affect one or more of the others. If this imbalance is left unaddressed for a long time, it can create a snowball effect, resulting in a vicious cycle that continually creates greater imbalance.

If your body is caught in this vicious cycle of imbalance, eliminating the stressors from your environment probably won't be enough to restore health. The only way to do that is to restore balance to the systems that have gone out of whack.

We cannot begin addressing these imbalances without first knowing which systems are out of balance. Again, there are specialty panels to help us identify these (listed in the prior chapter). These panels are not often recommended or used in a convention medical office, but they are essential for finding the underlying causes and what is needed to restore balance.

When I work with patients in this phase, my goal is to balance hormone levels, blood sugar, cortisol levels, gut bacteria, nutrients, neurotransmitters, and antioxidants. And as these systems balance, methylation improves and susceptibility to genetic tendencies decreases.

Once we know which systems need attention, restoring balance is often a two-step process. First, we would restore calming support in the body. For example, we would aim to lower cortisol levels if they are too high, or increase calming neurotransmitters, such as serotonin and GABA, if they are too low. We would also take steps to calm blood sugar fluctuations and reduce any inflammation in the body.

Once the body has "calmed down," we would start working on restoring natural stimulators like adrenaline and cortisol (if either is too low). These can help restore energy levels and mental focus.

It is essential to work on the calming support before introducing stimulating supplements, or you are likely to end up feeling worse. I'll guide you through this in upcoming chapters.

# STEP 3: Build Resilience

Once you have restored balance to your body's systems, your next aim should be to help your body maintain that balance, no matter what stress/stressors it might face in the future. This is what we mean by "resilience."

Resilience is the ability to go out into the world and bounce back when faced with things that may have made you sick in the past. It means your adrenal response is optimal, which, in turn, helps optimize your digestion, immune function, hormones, and neurotransmitters. When we are resilient, we get sick less often and recover more quickly. We become less susceptible to infection, allergens, and sensitivities.

In other words, the ultimate goal of my proprietary system is to help you STAY well, rather than make you feel "better" when your body is, essentially, unwell.

It can seem impossible. Stress surrounds us. Aging happens. But do we have to become less healthy and/or less happy as time and stress happen?

I don't believe so. And that's because I grew up learning that we can support our bodies to be healthy.

Then I trained in science, nutrition and naturopathic medicine to learn how to use foods, nutrients, herbs, and natural approaches to self-care in order to recover from and become resilient to stress.

It's not just about avoiding stress. That would be impossible. And actually, we need stress in order to thrive and accomplish our goals. It *is* a matter of supporting ourselves and our bodies through stress in order to keep up with stress and to maintain our health.

We also all have our unique genetic variations and tendencies. That's what makes us unique. We know our genetic tendencies are turned on by stress. The better we master and support ourselves under stress, the less we are susceptible to our genetic predispositions.

Amazing, right?

This is why I believe it's possible to be healthy and happy while stressed. And that is what I look forward to teaching you.

- - - - - - - - - - - - - - - - - - - - - - - - - - - - - - - - - - - - - - - - - -

## TAKE AWAY NOTES:

The three phases of recovery from stress:

1. _____

2. _____

3. _____

- - - - - - - - - - - - - - - - - - - - - - - - - - - - - - - - - - - - - - - - - -

# Section 2

## Recovering From Stress

# CHAPTER 5

# The Case of a High Performer

**D**avid: My wake-up call was my thyroid. I have Hashimoto's and my doctor wanted me to be on the thyroid support for life. I contacted you to see if there was a natural way to support the thyroid rather than the synthetic, daily pill they want me to take. In the process, I got actually more than I bargained for. I'm currently still taking thyroid support as you know, but the other diet changes and supplements, that you suggested based on my levels, are just making me feel so great. It's like a familiar feeling like how I used to feel twenty years ago. Like I said, I got a lot more than I bargained for because I was just looking to not take thyroid medications for the rest of my life, but in turn, I got my youth back.

Dr. Doni:  I love it. I love hearing that. And it has been relatively recent... a few weeks...that you started to make diet changes based on your IgA and IgG food sensitivities, and the supplements to help support your neurotransmitters to recover from stress, right? And already you're starting to feel different?

David: Night and day.

Dr. Doni: It's so great. I'm so happy for you. It's so exciting.

David: Yeah. You know it's funny because like you said, there are a lot of changes that I made in one shot. It's not just the supplements and diet. I've always felt strongly about getting good sleep, but you reinforced that. When I get your daily updates or sometimes you send them to me daily or sometimes I get them weekly, but I think it's good for the whole family. That's something that we really enjoy reading. I think the whole family needs to be more conscious of getting good sleep, eating more frequent meals, eating clean meals. The stuff that you say, like your little reminders, 'tip of the day' I call them, they're great. It's stuff that you know, but sometimes it takes a little reminder to remind you.

Dr. Doni: Yeah, just to be like, okay, make sure you try this today or try to get this in because there are so many different things that are going on. It's hard to juggle.

David: Can I just say something real quick?

Dr. Doni: Of course.

David: Because this is something that in my head, I'm going to start doing, and you may want to use it as an angle for your patients.

Dr. Doni: Oh, yeah, tell me more.

David: That is, when you're on the road, your first instinct is what is quick and easy to eat. Mickey D's or a slice of pizza. You should challenge yourself to find a healthy alternative. Just make it a game. Be like, you know what? Here I am in a city I've never been to, where can I eat that's really healthy? Because I notice that you do that.

Dr. Doni: Yes.

David: When you went to California, you were like, "Hey. Look what I found. I found a gluten free food truck."

Dr. Doni: Yes, that's true, that is what I do.

David: Tell your patients that too. Say, "When you're out of your comfort zone or you're not in your home town where you know places to eat ... Instead of just falling into what's easiest... Let me just get a quick burger or something quick and easy... challenge yourself to find the healthy choice."

Dr. Doni: That's a great idea. I do tend to often make things a game for myself. We may as well entertain ourselves and challenge ourselves a little bit and just be like, "Hey. Let me see what I can find." Because now it is often that you can find something gluten free somewhere.

David: Yes, yes.

Dr. Doni: It just takes that extra little reminder or mindset to go, "Oh yeah. I'm not just going to go straight to the place I usually eat. I'm going to find something different."

David: You know what? It's like going to the gym. It's not the easiest thing to get there, but when you're on your way home, you always feel good about being there.

Dr. Doni: Yeah. That's true. Once you're there, then you're like, "Thank goodness I got here."

David: Yeah. Same with eating well. When you wrap up a good meal, your body feels good, and you feel good. When you eat a slice of pizza or a burger, it just feels like it's just a lump in your stomach.

Dr. Doni: Now, do you find that these changes that you've been making, has it made a difference in your day-to-day life at your office? Like you said, it's already helping in your family too.

David: Yeah. I do find that I think a lot clearer. It's almost like the difference of functioning with a hangover as opposed to functioning with a good night's sleep. I feel like there's no fog, there's no haze. Everything is crystal clear. It's just easier to process things. It's easier to understand things. I do think that it helps when you're building your thought process. Don't you feel the same way?

Dr. Doni: Yeah, yeah. Just all of a sudden, things come easier. There is more efficiency.

David: Yes.

Dr. Doni: I've heard something similar from other people. They say "I can see things in my business or daily processes that I couldn't see before because my brain was just so foggy before."

David: Yes. "Foggy" is a perfect word to describe it... I don't feel like I was walking in a fog, but I do feel like since I have started your regimen, that things are a lot clearer.

Dr. Doni: That's outstanding. Have you noticed anything else that has shifted?

David: Now that you mention it, I may have a longer fuse. Instead of getting angry quicker, I may be a little bit more level that way. It takes a little bit more to get me angry.

Dr. Doni: I love it. The nutrients in the supplements you've been taking in the evening or bedtime can have a bit of a calming effect, so maybe you'll sleep better, but also remember that little by little over time, because they're nutrients, they are helping your body build back up your stress resilience.

David: Oh, really?

Dr. Doni: You get a short-term benefit of sleeping better at night, but over several months, you're building up your serotonin and your GABA, which are what I consider your stress buffer. When stress comes in, if we don't have enough stress buffer, we're vulnerable to the stress.

David: Right.

Dr. Doni: As you build up your stress buffer, and that will also help with that thing that you were mentioning where you feel like you have that little more space between you and a stress reaction.

David: Yes, yes.

Dr. Doni: That's what we want. We're building that stress buffer and that may be how you notice it, where you just feel like you have a little more space to be in stress.

David: Yeah. That must be working then!

Dr. Doni: I consider you already such a high performer. You run your own real estate company. You are a husband and a father. And like you said when you first came in to meet with me, you said, "I feel really well. Everything is good."

David: Yeah, but you know what? I remember what you said to me at that same meeting. You said, "What if it could be better? You may notice that things are even better." I remember hearing that and I was like, "How could they be?" You were right. They are. They did get better. It's wild. I didn't realize how things could change. You really, really helped me a lot and my wife is coming to meet with you soon too.

Dr. Doni: That's wonderful!

David: I talk to people and any time I talk to people I'm like, "Just go to Dr. Doni. Just listen to her," because I'm sure you don't have a one shoe-fits-all. I'm sure that each one of your patients requires a little fine tuning in whatever direction, but you are definitely ... You picked the perfect of line of career for what you're doing because I'm sure you're helping a lot of people, not just me.

Dr. Doni: Oh, thank you, thank you. It is. It's a passion for me. Sometimes people ask me why I do what I do, and it's hard for me to explain because this is just what I wake up thinking about.

David: Yeah.

Dr. Doni:    That's why I'm so excited to share more, write about this approach more and find more ways to share experiences like yours. I think it helps when people can hear a story and think, "Oh. I can relate to that person." That's why I'm so grateful for you sharing a bit of your story.

David:    If I had to say something that I could share that would relate to other people is it can get better. Believe it or not, you walk through life and you think this is normal. It's just like people who have an extra 10, 15 pounds. You don't have to be that way. I feel like my normal then was the old me. I don't think I'll ever go back to that. I still do get a craving for a burger here and there and I do. I'll give into that craving here and there, but I am so in tune to what I eat and how it makes me feel. It's funny. When we're done with a meal, it used to be like, how was that? Everything was about the taste, right? Now it's more like, how do you feel? How did that burger feel? How did that gluten free cracker feel? It's funny, when you're in tune with the way food makes you feel, you don't just go through life eating. You go through life eating for a purpose. You're like, I'm going to eat because I need nutrition. I'm going to eat because I need protein. I'm going to eat because I need my three-hour snack. I think you perceive eating in a whole different way once you start tuning into the way it makes you feel and what you're actually doing for your body.

50

Dr. Doni:   That's such a great point.

David:      It's not just hunger. It's like feeding your body. Not just ...Putting the food in. It has a purpose.

Dr. Doni:   That's such a good point. I always recommend learning as you go and having that body awareness and that's exactly what you're doing. Then you just say whatever you do have, if it's a burger, then you go, "Okay. How does that feel? Do I want to choose that every so often or do I want to choose something different?" Then you can go from there.

David:      Right, right, right. Well also, one of the things that I attribute success in whatever I do is I listen and I follow. If I'm going to ask somebody for advice, I'm going to follow that advice. When you tell me what to do, I'm doing it. There are very few things that I ignore. I think that as long as your patients are following your lead, you're going to put them down the right path.

Dr. Doni:   Sometimes we get hesitant to listen or to take in new information, but when you can listen and take it in and try it, and just see.

David:      Yes. Yeah.

Dr. Doni:   I think that's also a trait of a high performer. That's where you're willing to try new things and then see what works and move forward.

David:     Yes. I really feel like you're putting out a good service. I really do think it's the whole package Dr. Doni. It's the meeting you one on one, and then following up regularly to check in, and then reading and implementing your daily tips.

Dr. Doni:  Awesome. I'm so happy for you David.

# CHAPTER 6

# Address Leaky Gut and Inflammation

Perhaps you are now wondering: "what did David do to start feeling so much better?"

In the three phases of stress recovery, David was working in phases one and two. He had started to remove stressors, especially foods that are stressful for his body, and taking supplements to help rebalance nutrient levels, heal leaky gut and support calming neurotransmitters.

In this chapter, I'm going to tell you more about food sensitivities and leaky gut. This way you can start to implement the way David did. Then in the next chapter we'll cover rebalancing cortisol and neurotransmitters.

I invite you to start thinking: What foods could be a stress to your body? And, also, what effect does stress have on your digestion?

We're going to be looking at how stress affects your digestion because it has such a huge influence in the body. We know that when the digestion is stressed and inflamed, it sends stress signals throughout your body and nervous system. We'll also cover how stress causes leaky gut, how to look at food sensitivity results and what they can tell us, and how to heal leaky gut. And we will be discussing the gut bacteria (microbiome) because that's a key player here as well.

By understanding how stress affects your digestion, then you can help it recover from that stress exposure so that you can get the benefits of healthy digestion.

## Why Digestion First

We count on our digestion for digesting our food and absorbing our nutrients. The bacteria in our gut do all kinds of good jobs for us. We really need our digestion working and that's why we have to address it first thing. The truth is if we were to jump ahead and do anything else first, without addressing our gut, our digestion and our gut bacteria, we would just end up stalling and having to come back to this anyway.

I always figure better to start with the gut and digestion. Even if for example, you have an MTHFR genetic SNP or maybe even other health concerns, and maybe you don't even feel like you have a problem with your digestion. Even still, I'm always going to come to the digestion and address your gut health first, before moving on to anything else.

## How Stress Affects Digestion

The big picture view helps us to see that stress comes in and tells our adrenals to make cortisol and adrenaline. And that cortisol then goes out and affects several systems in our body, including the digestion as well as hormones, the immune system and the nervous system. There are a lot of hormones made in our digestion, and a majority of our immune system is located in our digestion. Plus, the nervous system is also very focused in our gut. Scientists have named the "gut-brain axis" because there's such a strong communication between the gut and the brain via hormones, the immune system and the nervous system.

So, really, when you think about it, stress affecting the gut has the biggest, potential impact on our health because it sends signals of stress throughout the body, including the nervous system. And, at the same time, by addressing gut health, we have the greatest potential for improved health.

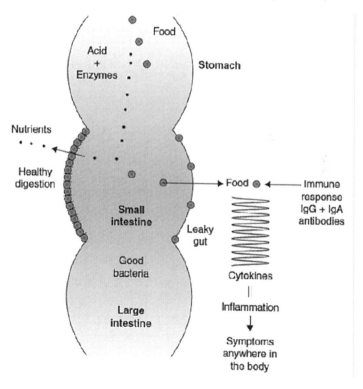

# What and Where is Leaky Gut

Sometimes it's hard to imagine what leaky gut is. People often ask, "what is leaky where?"

That is when I draw this diagram. It's almost looks like a little snowman where the top section is your stomach. After chewing food and swallowing, it goes to the stomach first, where protein is digested by stomach acid. Then it goes to the small intestine, where pancreatic enzymes and bile digest the food further. The large intestine is the last section.

We have cells lined up along the intestinal lining, making up the walls of our intestines. And those cells are so important. They do the final digestion of our food and they allow the nutrients through, either between them or actually through the cells, to get into our body. Otherwise, our nutrients from our food would just keep going down and through our intestines.

The way our food and nutrients actually get into our body is through these intestinal cells.

They are tiny cells, and so many of them. Imagine, if you were to spread out the small intestine, it would be as big as a tennis court. That's a lot of tiny intestinal cells! Inside our bodies the intestinal walls are all folded up. As food comes by, they digest it and then allow the nutrients to go across into your body.

Any undigested food or fiber continues down through your digestion where it feeds the bacteria. Now there's bacteria throughout out our digestive tract, but we're especially interested in the bacteria in the large intestine and feeding them because they do such important work for us. They make nutrients for us, and they communicate with our nervous system. So we really want those good bacteria as optimized as possible.

## What Happens with Stress

Now, when we're stressed, all of this gets thrown off track. We don't digest food as well. The intestinal cells that are so important to us get damaged. Usually our bodies are replacing them very frequently; every 72 hours, those cells are replaced. A whole tennis court worth is replaced constantly. But when we're under stress, it's like the tennis court gets broken up and worn out. It's because the body is using those same nutrients to help us deal with the stress, so it's not able to maintain the intestinal lining.

And then, if the gut bacteria get thrown out of balance, which it does when we are stressed, they create a lot of inflammation and that imbalanced gut bacteria then causes even more leaky gut. It is a snowball effect. Once one thing gets off track, it leads to the next thing going off track and the next thing going off track. And the next thing you know, it's what you see on the right side of this diagram, which is the cells are not as healthy as they should be. They're allowing undigested food to leak through. That's triggering an immune response because the immune system is trying to protect us from this food.

You see, the immune system is normally made to protect us from bacteria and viruses and foreign substances. Our immune system is used to seeing nutrients; it's not going to attack a nutrient. But when our immune system sees a piece of undigested food coming through, it's going to be really on top of it and start reacting. Say a little bit of protein, the immune system really goes after it with antibodies. Not only antibodies but the immune system also makes what are called cytokines and all kinds of inflammatory messengers.

We're going to talk about how we can do tests to identify what kind of immune responses are happening. But just think of it as the immune system just does a full attack trying to protect us from the food and it's really not the food's fault, it's that the intestinal lining is damaged and that's why it's triggering all of that inflammation.

The inflammation doesn't just stay in the digestive tract; that inflammation can go anywhere in the body. It can cause joint pains or headaches or runny nose and congestion or skin rashes or, you name it, that inflammation from the gut can cause symptoms anywhere in the body. And it's also known to trigger autoimmunity, so if you or someone you know has a form of autoimmunity, that means the immune system is now trying to protect the person from their own healthy cells. So not just trying to protect them from their food but if the immune system starts to try to protect from their healthy cells, that's called autoimmunity and it's linked to stress and leaky gut.

All of this disruption in the digestion also communicates to the stress system as a stress itself. Cortisol and the immune system triggers a whole response in the body that can lead to various symptoms. Even weight gain, diabetes and Alzheimer's disease are linked to this situation. That's why it's so important.

## Food Sensitivity

There's lots of different kinds of food sensitivity tests. It's pretty amazing, actually. They came up with this technology where they can basically match up the antibodies in our blood with foods. IgA and the IgG antibodies are really proteins in our bloodstream. And, foods have proteins as well, so what they're doing is essentially matching up the proteins. The machine can identify if you have an antibody to, let's say, whey, which is a dairy protein. This way we can really see what the immune system is up to.

In terms of these different antibodies, there are IgA and IgG and that is what I recommend checking when you do a food sensitivity panel. Sometimes people will do just IgG and that's okay because IgG is the most sneaky since it has the most delayed response. See the difference is that IgA reacts to foods over maybe a few days or a week after you eat the food and IgG reacts for up to three weeks after you eat the food. It's a long delay. This means that you might be eating these foods and not realizing that your immune system is reacting. The best option, however, is to check for both IgA and IgG reactions.

By the way, there's not, as far as I know, any particularly interesting way they named these antibodies; they just gave them a letter. Ig stands for immunoglobulin, which is another way of saying antibody. The other antibody we hear of often is IgE. IgE is involved when someone is allergic to peanuts and they end up in the emergency room or allergic to shrimp and they have an immediate and severe reaction, often causing them to not be able to breathe or tingling around the mouth. That immediate type of response is caused by IgE.

When you go to see an allergist, they specialize in IgE reactions only. They don't pay attention to IgA or IgG or any of the others (there's also IgM). If you are concerned about an immediate allergy response, then go to an allergist and be tested for IgE.

The food reactions that sneak up on us, especially in the situation of stress and leaky gut, are IgA and IgG. That is because they cause a delayed response, over days to weeks. It can be so subtle that you wouldn't know you are reacting. This is why a food sensitivity panel can be so helpful. It will clearly show which foods are triggering an inflammatory response and therefore which foods you want to avoid in order to help the leaky gut heal.

And that's what I'm most interested in. The question in my mind is always, "How are we going to heal leaky gut?" And the answer is, we can heal a leaky gut by avoiding the foods that are triggering really big antibody responses with

IgA and IgG. The reason I look at both of them is because they're not talking to each other. IgA might be reacting to different foods than the IgG. Sometimes they react to the same foods but it could be different. The only way to know is to check. Then we'll be adding the two together. They don't cancel each other out. They are both important, so think of it as adding the two reactions together.

When it comes to dairy, we are looking for reactions to the proteins in products made from cow milk. Casein and whey are the two proteins in dairy. Now usually we are thinking of the lactose in dairy but this is different than a lactose reaction because, when you think about it, the problem with lactose is *not* that it triggers the immune system; it's that lactose, for some people, is not getting digested very well. Lactose is a sugar and if you don't digest lactose very well, it can cause a lot of digestive upset because it can't be absorbed and is essentially stuck in your intestines, where it ends up being fermented by bacteria.

With IgA and IgG, the point is to identify which foods are triggering inflammation due to leaky gut. Generally, the understanding is the higher the antibody response, the more inflammation is being produced. Those are the most important foods to avoid. You would also want to decrease your exposure to moderately reactive foods because those foods are also triggering inflammation and it helps to create more variety in your diet while we heal leaky gut. Even with the low reactive foods, I usually say to just try to rotate them. Don't eat the same food every day. It's when we eat the same foods every day that it's more likely going to leak through and trigger the immune system.

I want to emphasize that gluten is the only exception to this because with gluten, even when it has a low reaction, it's still a positive gluten reaction. I've figured this out over years of reviewing food sensitivity panels and thousands of results: Gluten can cause trouble even at a low reaction. I've had patients where they've had extreme symptoms. We're talking headaches and dizziness and feeling terrible, and they only have a low reaction. The other thing that can happen is, say, you've already been decreasing the amount of gluten in your diet, and you do a food sensitivity panel, then you might only show as a low gluten because you're not exposed to it as much. But it's still a gluten sensitivity. What we call a non-celiac gluten sensitivity (NCGS).

And what I do is I look not just at the gluten, but also at the other grains that contain gluten. Barley contains gluten; so does rye, spelt and wheat. We're looking for a gluten pattern, and when we see that, we know, that's a gluten sensitivity.

To clarify, these IgA and IgG panels cannot be used to diagnose Celiac disease because celiac is when the antibodies start reacting to the intestinal cells in addition to reacting to gluten. We would need to do a different type of test to know whether a person has Celiac disease, which is an autoimmune condition. Currently the standard for diagnosing Celiac is an intestinal biopsy to identify damage to the intestinal cells. A person with Celiac will likely be highly reactive to gluten on IgA and IgG, and when you think about it, the treatment for Celiac disease and gluten sensitivity is the same. For both of them, the treatment is to avoid gluten.

## Why am I Reacting to Foods I Eat Often

The thing to remember is the food you're eating often is more likely to leak through and trigger the immune system. To me that is an exact definition of leaky gut. It means that the foods are coming through, they're not getting digested well, they're leaking right through the intestinal wall, and triggering the immune system. We're going to need to not only eliminate those foods, but work hard to get those intestinal cells recovering.

By the time the intestinal cells are damaged with leaky gut, you're likely not even getting the nutrients from your food because the food isn't getting digested; it's just leaking through and triggering an immune response.

So, when you react to food you're eating often, that's the definition of leaky gut. But it's not necessarily all the food you eat often; that's why doing a food sensitivity panel is helpful so you can really see which foods your immune system has identified. There's no way to anticipate that. Every person's immune system has an agenda of its own. The only way to know which foods are an issue for you is to test and find out what's going on in there.

## What Causes Leaky Gut

We talked about how stress causes leaky gut but, I want to make sure to mention that gluten itself causes leaky gut. Which is why gluten is such a trouble causer. Not only can you start to become sensitive to gluten, but the gluten actually causes the leaky gut. It actually opens up the spaces between those cells using a substance called zonulin, and that creates leaky gut.

Even when a person is reacting to fruits and nuts, it's not really the fruits and the nuts that were the problem. It's likely that gluten caused the leaky gut, along with stress and some other factors. And that's what then leads to more and more reactions to more foods; gluten is causing that leaky gut issue to perpetuate. In some cases, these additional food reactions are referred to as "gluten-mimicking" because they are associated with gluten.

Alcohol can also cause leaky gut. So can caffeine. Sugar definitely. Stress we talked about. And certain medications like antibiotics; proton-pump inhibitors, which are used for treating reflux; and many other medications can increase leaky gut. Also, not just emotional stress but physical trauma can cause leaky gut as well.

As you start to think about it, basically all of us have some degree of leaky gut because we're exposed to these very things. Even toxins in our environment and pesticides on food cause leaky gut. It turns out it is more a matter of *how severe is the leaky gut* at this point in time and what can we do to help it recover.

## What's the Trouble with Gluten

I wanted to touch on gluten a little bit more specifically. We talk about gluten as if it's a single thing. But gluten is actually made up of a whole bunch of tiny proteins. They're grouped into two types: gliadin and glutenin. When we look closely at gliadin, we'll find there are sections of gliadin that our body, human bodies, cannot digest. Nobody. No humans can digest this part of gluten. If we are exposed to small amounts of it, it's okay. But if we get exposed to a lot and every meal, then at some point in time, it could cause leaky gut and our immune system could try to protect us from it. And that's what triggers gluten sensitivity and Celiac disease.

We also know that there's certain genetic tendencies to react to gluten. I think of it as if a person immune system has a catcher's mitt made for reacting to gluten. Every time they consume gluten, their immune system is watching for it and goes right after it. It is the HLA-DQ2 and DQ8 genes that are associated with gluten sensitivity and Celiac disease

## Testing for Leaky Gut

There are different tests available to check for leaky gut. It can be tested through saliva, urine or blood. They can also test for zonulin in stool and blood. These tests do exist and sometimes are helpful to see. But what I find is that by doing an IgA and IgG food panel, we can get a sense of the degree of leaky gut based on the severity and number of reactions to foods. Plus, with a food sensitivity panel, we also get information about which foods are most important to avoid in order to help heal the leaky gut. So we get both pieces of information: how severe is the leaky gut and which foods to avoid in order to heal it faster.

## How to Heal Leaky Gut

When we think about the nutrients and herbs that help intestinal cells, we need to consider what I think of as the paradox of healing leaky gut. When leaky gut is more severe, we actually have to start with simpler approaches and single ingredients. Sometimes we need to start with plain glutamine powder or maybe glutamine with DGL (deglycyrrhizinated licorice). We have to start very simple because the more reactive the immune system in the gut, the more likely you would even react to herbs and natural substances.

As leaky gut heals, then we can add in other herbs. We might be able to add in aloe or slippery elm, marshmallow root and quercetin. For mild leaky gut, we can start off with combination products from the start.

Here is my overall strategy for healing leaky gut:

1. Avoid the most reactive foods, and minimize exposure to lower reactive foods

2. Take digestive enzymes when you eat, and by doing that we prevent new reactions

3. Use nutrients and herbs to help heal intestinal cells and heal leaky gut

4. Optimize good bacteria

Let's talk this through in more detail. We talked about food sensitivity results and avoiding the most reactive foods, as well as gluten, so you have that part.

To support digestion, in addition to taking time to sit and chew while you eat, I recommend taking plant-based pancreatic enzymes with meals. Pancreatic enzymes can help digest proteins, fats and carbohydrates, ensuring that you can absorb the nutrients and avoid immune responses to the foods you eat. An example product that I recommend is called Enzyme Support.

When it comes to the nutrients and herbs to help with healing the intestinal cells, the first in line is glutamine. It is an amino acid that is important fuel for intestinal cells. They require glutamine to survive. The next I would choose is DGL, or herbal licorice. It's not the same as the candy licorice. It's the herb licorice that's been deglycyrrhizinated, which means the part that can increase blood pressure has been removed. That's the great thing about DGL: even if your blood pressure is a concern, you can still take DGL to help heal leaky gut.

From there, you might choose quercetin, aloe, slippery elm, and/or curcumin, separately or in combination. We could also add MSM (methylsulfonylmethane), which provides sulfur that helps the tight junctions between the cells to heal and zinc which is essential for healthy new cells in the intestinal lining. I find most patients do best with a powder that includes a few of these ingredients, to start, because it is easy to add to a protein shake and doesn't tend to cause reactions. I recommend Leaky Gut Support powder. (See Resources section for information about recommended products)

And the final step for healing leaky gut is all about getting your healthy bacteria balanced so they can help heal and prevent leaky gut. That's what we'll cover in the next chapter.

# CHAPTER 7

# Optimizing Gut Bacteria

It can be hard to imagine that the bacteria in your intestines (referred to as your microbiome or microbiota) have anything to do with your joint pain, anxiety, blood sugar levels, immune system, or menstrual cycle – let alone your mood, behavior, and focus. It is definitely not something you're likely to hear about when you meet with your primary care doctor, gastroenterologist, neurologist, psychiatrist, or any other medical specialist for that matter. It has simply not been integrated into standard medical care yet.

I say "yet" because I believe that over the next decade (or two), addressing gut microbiota particularly for anxiety, depression, Alzheimer's disease and other neurodegenerative diseases, autism, and pain will become universal. That is because there is such a huge amount of research being done.

In fact, the US National Institute of Mental Health (NIMH) in Bethesda, Maryland has funded seven pilot studies to investigate the **microbiota-gut-brain axis**. And the US Office of Naval Research in Arlington, Virginia plans to spend $14.5 million over the next 5-6 years examining the gut's role in cognitive function and stress responses.

## Inflammation Signal

Well, in simple terms, the bacteria in your gut communicate with the rest of your body by producing substances, triggering inflammatory messages and/or by sending signals via your nerves. If or when the balance of bacteria is disrupted, that has the potential to send a very different message to your nervous system and influence your mood, memory, and focus. Your metabolism and likelihood of gaining weight is also affected, but for now let's focus on your nervous system.

It was previously thought that the nervous system is protected by the blood-brain-barrier (BBB), but now we understand that inflammatory messages from your gut can be communicated *across* the BBB. In other words, inflammation from the digestive tract can spread inflammation throughout your body including your nervous system. I call it "inflamed brain." This is why, if you get a stomach virus, your whole body feels unwell.

Two (perhaps surprising) examples are **ANXIETY AND DEPRESSION**, WHICH ARE NOW KNOWN TO BE CAUSED BY INFLAMMATION IN YOUR NERVOUS SYSTEM.

Other common symptoms in their brain due to inflammation that came from the gut are:

- Brain fog
- Difficulty focusing

- Obsessive Compulsive Disorder
- Forgetfulness
- Worries and fears
- Repeating thoughts
- Restless sleep

## Other Ways Bacteria Signal Stress

In addition to inflammation from the gut, the bacteria in your gut produce substances – some considered good and protective, such as butyrate, and others not-so-good, known as LPS (lipopolysaccharide) – that cross your intestinal lining and travel throughout your body.

But the connection goes beyond inflammation and substances; these bacteria are actually able to send signals to your genes telling them to turn on or off pathways that influence certain functions such as the production of serotonin and Brain-Derived Neurotrophic Factor (BDNF), both of which effect your mood and focus.

Just as an imbalance of bacteria could be detrimental, optimizing the desired bacteria could be beneficial. But you also don't want too much good bacteria. I'll get into that more soon.

Another communication route between your gut and your brain (and other areas of your body) is via your vagal nerve. This important nerve sends signals from your brain (your nervous system) to your digestion and back again.

71

If there is stress (such as inflammation or an imbalance of bacteria) then a *stress signal* is sent from your gut telling the rest of your body to respond. That response could lead to a number of symptoms including nausea, reflux, difficulty swallowing, muscle spasms, anxiety, racing heart, frequent urination, fatigue, faintness, and/or tinnitus (ringing in your ears).

Each person experiences the microbiota-gut-brain axis differently. For some, it takes a major change in the bacteria to result in health issues. Others will notice a headache, mood change, brain fog or joint pain after even the slightest diet change or stress.

This variation is at least partially determined by your genetics (as well as that of your ancestors) and your exposure to stress (even in childhood), or what I think of as your susceptibilities.

## What Disrupts the Microbiota?

Psycho-emotional stress, sugar, and gluten (in anything made from wheat, rye, barley or spelt) are all well-established causes of a disruption in your gut flora, which is why I refer to all of them as *stresses*. When you are stressed, the stress hormone cortisol sends signals to decrease activity in the digestive tract and increase activity to your muscles and brain.

If you are stressed a lot of the time, you will not digest food well, be prone to intestinal permeability (known as LEAKY GUT), and the balance of bacteria in your gut will be disrupted.

Some bacteria will overgrow and others will undergrow, leading to increased inflammation and further damage to the intestinal lining.

Then the part of your immune system that sits under the intestinal lining becomes activated and starts sending signals to the rest of the immune system, both locally and throughout your body. The immune system also sends stress messages back to your brain, indicating to your central nervous system that there is even more stress and disruption to the bacteria (dysbiosis).

It becomes a vicious cycle of "internal stress."

The over-use of antibiotics (such as for sinus, dental, skin or bladder infections) is another top way that microbiota are thrown off track, so preventing the use of antibiotics and other medications that disrupt those bacteria is a priority for healing and preventing this situation.

## What Can You Do To Protect Your Microbiome?

Anything you can do to fight off infections through diet, sleep, nutrients, and herbs will protect your microbiome, which in my mind is essentially the greatest health prevention tactic you could implement. To learn how to recover from a cold virus without antibiotics, refer to the articles in the Resources section.

The microbiota is also affected by a number of other things. Avoiding and addressing these substances and issues will help keep you and your microbiota in good health:

- Proton Pump Inhibitors – used to treat GERD Read more about my approach to GERD in the Resources section.
- Alcohol
- Lack of fiber – such as in a diet filled with processed foods
- Food poisoning or traveler's diarrhea

## Can You Test Your Microbiome?

There are labs that offer specialized **stool testing** that tells us what is going on with your gut bacteria based on the DNA of the bacteria. They show us patterns of 'dysbiosis' – imbalanced bacteria – and identify the bacteria that are present in your gut based on their DNA, which is rather amazing. They can also give an indication of how well you are digesting food and whether inflammation is present.

Some of these stool panels are more clinical – and you'll need to work with a naturopathic doctor to access them. Others, such as Viome and Ubiome, are available direct to consumer and while they don't provide all the information that the clinical panels do, they will give you a sense of whether you need to pay more attention to your gut bacteria.

## How to Optimize Your Microbiome

Over the years I've seen thousands of patients with varying degrees of dysbiosis and through that process I've learned that there are basically 3 categories of disruption that each require a different approach:

1. **Mild disruption** usually just requires consistent dosing of a HIGH-QUALITY LACTOBACILLUS AND BIFIDO PROBIOTIC PRODUCT, along with diet changes (avoiding gluten and sugar), DIGESTIVE ENZYMES and HERBS/NUTRIENTS TO HEAL LEAKY GUT and get things back to balance again.

2. **Moderate disruption** means you probably feel okay most days, but just when you think you're doing all right, pain, bloating and bowel irregularity remind you that you're just not feeling your best. You can start in with digestive support, but if you feel worse, you'll want to slow down until your body has healed a bit and is ready for more support.

   **Avoiding foods that increase inflammation** (which may include foods that trigger HISTAMINE, such as aged meats and fermented foods) and completing a genetic stool analysis (and possibly also a breath test) to determine the best probiotic for you will help the healing process. Some "probiotics" can actually trigger histamine, so be careful.

   Digestive enzymes to ensure food is being digested and anti-inflammatory herbs, such as DGL (licorice), slippery elm (ulmus) and/or marshmallow (althea) may all help balance things out again.

   When a stool panel shows an overgrowth of bacteria, I guide patients through a process of using herbal extracts that kill the overgrowing bacteria (or yeast) while using specialized bacteria in capsule form that can actually act as traffic directors, directing the overgrowing bacteria to go, and the good bacteria to stay.

3. **Severe disruption** presents something of a paradox in that you need to start with *less* treatment when you have *more*. This is because your digestive system is so reactive you'll likely react to anything that we add to your regime. So the goal is to start out with the "safest" low-reactivity foods and products until things settle down enough that we can start to treat.

In many severe cases, we need to work gradually and carefully to get rid of unhealthy or overgrowing bacteria and/or yeast using herbal extracts before adding in classic probiotics containing lactobacillus and bifidobacteria.

There are new, innovative ways to do this, including fecal transplants – a method of introducing stool from a healthy person in order to transfer a more optimal set of bacteria. This approach has been established as effective especially in the case of *antibiotic-resistant c. difficile infection*. This type of treatment is already available in other countries and could become more available for other conditions (such as anxiety and depression) in the U.S, in the near future.

All of this is very good news for healthcare but it is still not as simple as it may seem. This is why there are hundreds of studies currently under way, looking at which bacteria you want in your microbiome and which you don't, and which forms of can shift things in the right direction.

## Essential to Heal Your Gut and Rebalance Your Response to Stress

Basically, regardless of the severity of your dysbiosis, we need to heal the environment in your gut, and decrease inflammation, while also supporting digestion, feeding healthy bacteria and ensuring regular bowel movements.

You'll want to do a FOOD SENSITIVITY PANEL to find out exactly which foods to avoid. You may need to rely on protein shakes, such as my ALL-IN-ONE PEA PROTEIN SHAKE, or a single ingredient shake or even amino acid powder (in more severe cases) to get nutrition while your gut heals.

Be sure to turn to the resources section of this book for the health panels and products I recommend.

It's quite a complex system that works best when we are the least stressed. In fact, you can start to support your digestion by simply taking a few deep breaths before you start eating, then chewing well, and enjoying your food – all of which ensures your nervous system encourages the whole system to work well.

# CHAPTER 8

# Rebalance Cortisol and Adrenal Function

**I** want to emphasize that stress affects each of us differently. How it affects you is all down to your personal genetics and stress exposure, starting early in life. That is why I recommend actually doing a health panel to find out your current cortisol levels throughout the day and your adrenaline levels.

The combination of these two factors - genetic and stress exposure - create what I refer to as your "STRESS FINGERPRINT" I believe that understanding your stress fingerprint leads to self-acceptance.

Knowing how our genes and our personal history have designed a blueprint for our health tendencies helps us accept our whole selves and work with what we have. It enables us to make choices to support our bodies correctly, and make the appropriate lifestyle changes that help us feel well in the long term.

Because everyone's stress fingerprint is different, there is no cookie-cutter solution for adrenal distress.

For example, licorice (the herb, not the candy) is often helpful when cortisol levels are low because it supports cortisol production. However, if your cortisol levels are too high, licorice would not be an appropriate choice. Instead, I might recommend ashwagandha root, as it can help lower cortisol.

In my experience, people trying to heal themselves from adrenal issues may try taking a few vitamins or herbs, but they may not be using the nutrients and herbs their body really needs. My research shows that we cannot go by symptoms alone to determine the best approach to adrenal function. We need to measure the levels in order to know how stress has affected your body specifically.

Another pattern I see is that people are often unaware of the best order to introduce products to obtain the desired result. For example, I find it is extremely important and more efficient to calm the nervous system and decrease elevated adrenaline and cortisol BEFORE supporting the adrenal glands to make more cortisol and adrenaline.

First thing first, our focus is on getting you out of "stress mode." A few nutrients that help support a calm nervous system include:

Magnesium

Vitamin B6

Glycine

Theanine

GABA

To decrease cortisol that is too high, herbs and nutrients to consider are:

Ashwaganda

Phosphatidylserine

Banaba leaf

Magnolia root

If you have a sense or know that your adrenal function has been affected by stress, and you're not sure where to start, think "start with calming support." Include calming activities, such as:

Meditation

Mindfulness

Listen to music

Take a walk or stretch

Breathe

Call a friend

Get a massage

And it's always important to listen to your body: what feels good, what doesn't. Choose more of what feels good.

Once you're out of "stress mode" and elevated cortisol and adrenaline levels have been addressed, then you can add in support to increase cortisol and/or adrenaline if your levels are low in the morning. In most cases, I aim to accomplish this type of support using nutrients and herbs. I prefer for your adrenal glands to function well on their own.

If, however, your adrenals are quite depleted and not able to produce more cortisol, then we may need to temporarily use cortisol from an animal source (or synthetic) in order to fill in for your adrenals while they recover. The goal is to transition from glandular cortisol support to nutrient and herbal support within a few weeks or months.

In most cases, it *is* possible to recover from adrenal distress **naturally**, without taking prescription medications or even glandular cortisol. However, working with an experienced naturopathic doctor is **essential** to determining exactly how stress is affecting your adrenal response system, and which nutrients and herbs you need to correct your unique stress fingerprint.

In summary, here are 5 guidelines I've learned to follow after helping thousands of patients (and myself) recover from adrenal distress:

1. **Address elevated cortisol levels**. If these levels are elevated, the first step is to use nutrients, herbs, and mindfulness techniques to address your stress response and get those levels closer to optimal.

2. **Match your doses to your unique cortisol pattern**, *e.g.* if your cortisol increases after 7 pm, take nutrients and herbs that help decrease cortisol by about 6 pm.

3. **Know and address your adrenaline (norepinephrine and epinephrine) levels** in addition to cortisol. If you only address cortisol, you'll be missing part of the solution. If you do have elevated adrenaline (norepinephrine and/or epinephrine), the nutrients to consider first are magnesium and vitamin B6 because they help your body to process adrenaline.

   Knowing your genetic SNPs can be very helpful and addressing methylation will be essential to maintaining optimal adrenaline levels long term.

4. Always **ensure that you have enough calming support before adding stimulation support**. Even if you feel tired, if you add in support for low cortisol and/or adrenaline before you have enough calming neurotransmitters, like serotonin and GABA, then you risk feeling worse. Learn about balancing neurotransmitters in the next chapter.

5. **When ready to support low cortisol and/or adrenaline, start slowly**, and only increase to the dose that feels best to your body. My rule is: If you feel worse when you start taking a nutrient or herb (or medication, for that matter), it is best to **stop and check in with your naturopathic doctor or practitioner**.

The overall goal is to support your body to achieve optimal levels so that healthy signals will be sent out to the rest of your body, which can then help reciprocate the message, helping your body to achieve a renewed balanced state. At this point you'll also be more resilient to stress in the future. And you'll be more aware of what to do and what to take to keep your adrenal function optimal.

Be sure to refer to the resources section of this book for product recommendations from me.

**NOTE:** If you have been diagnosed with **Addison's or Cushing's Disease** (extreme forms of adrenal distress), it is important that you follow the recommendations of your endocrinologist. You *will* likely need to take prescription medications, but you could work with a naturopathic doctor to determine whether you could additionally benefit from nutrients and herbs.

# Section 3

Becoming Resilient to Stress

# CHAPTER 9

# Rebalance Neurotransmitters

**W**e often led to believe that depression, anxiety, and difficulties with sleep and mental focus are all caused by low serotonin levels (although sometimes that is part of the issue), and that the only way to address these problems is to take anti-depressant or anti-anxiety medication.

Then, if one pill fails to work, we can add another, and another after that. Even when we don't feel any better – and even when we experience some pretty scary side effects – we persist with the medication, because we have been told we will get worse without it. Essentially, the message we have been told is that having mental health problems means our bodies are "broken." And at no point are neurotransmitter levels measured.

But as someone who has studied science from a young age – including the science of food nutrients, biochemistry, and psychoneuroimmunology – depression and anxiety is not caused by a deficiency of anti-depressant medications. Depression is not always caused by low serotonin levels.

What's more, anti-depressants don't address the underlying issues, and could make you feel worse.

On the other hand, there is so much we can do to measure and balance neurotransmitters using nutrients and herbs. The nervous system is not a mystery. We can understand it, support it, and help our bodies recover.

**Essentially, there is far more to the story of mental health than what we have been led to believe.**

To see the full picture, we need to understand the **science behind neurotransmitters** – how they work in our bodies, how they influence our mood and mental focus, and how we can bring them into balance *naturally*.

## What Are Neurotransmitters?

Neurotransmitters are naturally produced chemicals that our bodies use to send messages between nerves. That's why I like to call them "messengers." Our moods are profoundly affected by how efficiently these messengers communicate throughout our nervous system.

Other messengers in the body include hormones (which communicate messages between organs), and cytokines (which communicate messages within the immune system).

Some messengers fall into more than one category, as they communicate across more than system of the body. HISTAMINE IS ONE EXAMPLE: its primary function is to act as messenger in the immune system, but it also communicates with the nervous system. That's why allergies can sometimes make you feel irritable. I mention this to illustrate how the systems in our bodies are interconnected, and how what goes on in one system can affect another.

## Calming vs. Stimulating Neurotransmitters

Broadly speaking, there are two kinds of neurotransmitter: Those that **calm**, and those that **stimulate**. Ideally, we want a balance of the two.

During the day, we want our bodies to produce more stimulating neurotransmitters than calming. Conversely, we want our bodies to produce more calming neurotransmitters at night, so we can sleep soundly. When we are under stress, however, we want our bodies to make both: stimulating neurotransmitters to help us think quickly, and calming neurotransmitter to help us recover from the stress.

All neurotransmitters – whether calming or stimulating – affect our mood, energy, focus, sleep, and memory. Too much or too little of ANY neurotransmitter can lead to health issues. Some of the most important are:

- **Serotonin** is a calming neurotransmitter. Best known for how it affects mood, serotonin is also essential for thought processes, dreaming, and *appetite.* In fact, **most of your serotonin is made in the gut**; so, if you have chronic digestive problems, it is likely to affect your serotonin levels.

- **GABA (gamma-aminobutyric acid)** is also a calming neurotransmitter. I call GABA our "stress buffer," as it helps counter our exposure to stress with calmness. When we are exposed to chronic stress, GABA can become depleted, which makes it more difficult to recover from the negative effects of stress, and more prone to feeling out of balance overall.

- **Glutamate** is an extremely stimulatory neurotransmitter that helps us think, learn, and remember. Think of it as the opposite of GABA. In fact, our bodies can convert GABA to glutamate, and vice versa, working hard to attain an optimal balance of stimulation and calmness. When glutamate becomes out of balance and elevated, it is considered a "neurotoxin," leading to such negative effects as seizures, migraines, and insomnia.

- **Dopamine** is also stimulating, and known mainly for its role in our ability to experience pleasure. But dopamine is also active in determining mood, movement, and mental processing. Dopamine is converted into adrenaline, in amounts determined by stress exposure, nutrient levels, methylation function, and our overall genetics. Low levels of dopamine are associated with conditions such as Tourette's Syndrome and Parkinson's disease.

- **Adrenaline** (which includes norepinephrine and epinephrine) is a stimulatory neurotransmitter. Adrenaline kicks in when we need a burst of energy, strength, and power, causing our hearts to beat faster and our bodies to sweat, as well as affecting mood and mental focus. Adrenaline is produced by both the nervous system and the adrenal glands, as part of our stress response. With exposure to long-term stress, adrenaline can become depleted, which can lead to chronic fatigue.

As you can see, there are many other neurotransmitters besides serotonin that influence our mood. Depression and other mood-related issues could be the result of an imbalance of any one of these.

Moreover, as all our bodily systems communicate with one another, they could also be affected by an imbalance in our hormones (such as cortisol and thyroid hormones), internal inflammation, digestive issues, and/or blood sugar irregularities.

## How Does the Body Make Neurotransmitters?

I really want to emphasize one thing: **Our bodies MAKE neurotransmitters. They don't come from pills.**

However, to help our bodies make all the neurotransmitters we need for optimal mood and overall health, we need to ensure we give them the necessary nutrients from our diet, including:

1.  **Protein** (whether animal or vegetarian) is the first ingredient our body needs to make neurotransmitters is protein. Protein contains amino acids. Two examples of amino acids are **tryptophan** (one of the building blocks of serotonin) and **tyrosine** (one of the building blocks of dopamine and adrenaline).

    Thus, if we don't eat enough protein, *with a wide variety of amino acids,* our bodies won't have what they need to make neurotransmitters. Also keep in mind that when we are stressed, we don't digest protein as well, and when leaky gut exists, we don't absorb amino acids effectively. All of this leads to depleted neurotransmitters.

2.  **Minerals.** For the body to convert amino acids into neurotransmitters, it needs specific nutrients. Minerals like **magnesium, zinc, and iron** are all integral to the process.

3.  **B-vitamins.** B-vitamins play many roles in neurotransmitter production, as well as in helping to break them down (neurotransmitters are constantly made and broken down).

    Vitamin B6, for example, is essential in the production of serotonin, dopamine, and norepinephrine. To break down neurotransmitters so they do not become toxic, our bodies use the "METHYLATION CYCLE "(click to read an article explaining methylation), which brings folate and B12 together to make SAM (S-adenosyl methionine). SAM is then used by the body to make and break down neurotransmitters. If methylation is stuck, our neurotransmitters are affected.

**The bottom line is this:** By giving our bodies what they need, they are more able to produce (and break down) the neurotransmitters we need for optimal mood, energy, sleep, memory, and mental focus. I

know that, after all we've been told by the pharmaceutical industries, it might seem unimaginable that FOOD holds the key to resolving so many mental health problems. But I assure you, every one of our physical processes – including mental health – rests upon a foundation of proper nutrition, as well as recovery and resilience to stress.

## How Do Neurotransmitters Get Out of Balance?

**Stress** is the most critical factor in neurotransmitter balance. This is because our bodies are designed to *modify* the production of neurotransmitters whenever we are exposed to any kind of stress.

"Stress" can be caused by any number of things, including:

- Emotional and/or physical abuse or trauma
- Life changes, such as deaths in the family or divorce
- Financial and work stress

- Consuming unhealthy food substances, such as high fructose corn syrup, MSG, and food additives

- Substance abuse and/or excess consumption of alcohol, caffeine, or sugar

- Gluten, which is known to trigger an inflammatory response in the body that leads to imbalanced neurotransmitters

- Exposure to pesticides, herbicides, pollution, chemicals (such as in personal care and cleaning products), or heavy metals – all of these can impair the proper production and breakdown of neurotransmitters

- Oxidative stress, due to chronic infection, inflammation, and insufficient anti-oxidants

- Digestive issues, including imbalanced bacteria in the intestines (known as dysbiosis), leaky gut (intestinal permeability), poor digestion, and malabsorption (inability to absorb nutrients well)

As it is impossible to be alive without encountering some form of stress, our neurotransmitters are part of a continual balancing act. This means that **all of us are at risk of developing a neurotransmitter imbalance** at some point in our lives.

Some people may also have GENETIC TENDENCIES that can cause their neurotransmitters to become imbalanced more easily. Our chances of developing an imbalance increase if we are exposed to multiple forms of stress and/or our stress continues for a prolonged period. In such scenarios, the systems of the body struggle to recover until the stress triggers are eliminated.

## How Prescription Drugs Affect Neurotransmitters

Many people are under the impression that anti-depressant prescription medications increase serotonin levels, but this is not actually the case. To understand why, we need to look at how neurotransmitters function in the nervous system.

When neurotransmitters go between one nerve and the next, they connect via "receptors" and "transport proteins." There are specific receptors/proteins for each type of neurotransmitter, and for moving neurotransmitters in and out of nerve cells, and our bodies can modify the amount of each type of receptor.

Prescription medications work by **binding to the receptors/proteins**. For example, SSRIs (selective serotonin reuptake inhibitors) work by binding to a transport protein (SERT) which then *inhibits* serotonin from being broken down.

By preventing its "reuptake," SSRIs leave more serotonin to be active. This means, while it keeps your serotonin around longer, it does nothing to increase serotonin. If your levels happen to be too low, they will remain low.

As SSRIs influence your nerve receptors, they can cause many long-lasting, negative effects, including drug dependency and withdrawal symptoms, if/when you stop (or decrease the dose of) your medication. Other known side effects include weight gain and change in libido.

Ironically (and tragically), they can also cause decreased memory, increased anxiety and depression, and even suicidal thoughts – symptoms people had hoped to eliminate by taking these medications in the first place. Sadly, when one medication fails to give patients the hoped-for relief from their symptoms, most conventional doctors will simply prescribe another to take its place, which only perpetuates the problem, sometimes for many years.

It is easy to understand how, when given no other option, patients often end up feeling stuck, dependent, and afraid to come off their prescription meds. Furthermore, because these medications actually alter the chemistry of your brain, stopping "cold turkey" is not recommended, as it is likely to result in severe withdrawal symptoms.

Coming off the meds should only be done under the guidance of your prescribing doctor as well as a qualified, experienced health practitioner – preferably a naturopathic doctor – who will measure your neurotransmitter levels, and can support you to identify and address the stresses (*listed above*) affecting your neurotransmitters PRIOR to decreasing any medication doses.

# Depression Is Not Always the Result of Low Serotonin

It is not a foregone conclusion that someone experiencing depression or mood issues has low serotonin, or that low serotonin levels are the ONLY issue causing these problems.

A patient might have problems in the production and/or metabolism (breakdown) of other neurotransmitters, as well. Depression can also be caused by high or low cortisol levels. Irregular cortisol can, in turn, increase the likelihood of digestive issues and inflammation in the digestive tract, which can also cause low mood, anxiety and brain fog via what's known as the gut-brain axis. Low thyroid function is yet another potential cause.

Because it would be wrong to assume serotonin is the problem, even if you, as a patient, were taking prescription medication for depression, I would run a full range of tests and health panels to get a comprehensive picture of what is really going on, including:

- **A blood test** to check for anemia and low thyroid function, as well as B-vitamin levels, methylation (homocysteine), blood sugar levels (HbgA1c), iron levels (ferritin), and possibly other things, depending on your case.

- **A saliva or urine panel** to measure your cortisol levels throughout the day. This way, we can determine the best approach to optimize your cortisol.

- **A urinary neurotransmitter panel,** which can tell us your serotonin, GABA, dopamine, and adrenaline levels so we know which **neurotransmitters** are too low or too high, and where your metabolism is getting stuck.

- **An IGA AND IGG FOOD SENSITIVITY PANEL,** to determine whether you have a gluten sensitivity, dairy protein sensitivity, or reactions to other foods you eat, as well as to identify the severity of leaky gut. Any of these factors can contribute to inflammation, which may be affecting your neurotransmitter balance via the gut-brain axis.

- **A full genetic panel** that enables me to analyze genes, such as MTHFR, COMT and MAO related to methylation, neurotransmitter processing, and how your body responds to stress.

- **A nutrient panel,** to see if there are any deficiencies that may be impairing proper neurotransmitter function.

- **I also often recommend doing a urine panel for organic acids,** which are metabolites that tell us about mitochondrial function, oxidative stress, methylation, and nutrient use in your cells.

# 4 Key Ways to Rebalance Neurotransmitters Naturally

With the information gathered from testing, you and your health practitioner can create a plan for dietary and lifestyle changes that can help get your body back to optimal production and breakdown of neurotransmitters, and hopefully get you to the point where you and your doctor feel you are ready to wean yourself away from anti-depressants or other prescription medications.

The **natural** approach to restoring optimal neurotransmitter production and processing can be summed up in four strategies:

1. **DIETARY CHANGES** – based on your food sensitivities and blood sugar levels.

2. **NUTRITIONAL SUPPLEMENTS** – vitamins, minerals, amino acids, etc., depending on what we discover from your results.

3. **BETTER SLEEP** – sleep is when your body recovers from any kind of imbalance. Depression and anxiety often come with disrupted sleep. Making sure you sleep better is an essential part of the healing equation. With or without depression, if sleep is an issue for you, you might wish to have a look at my bestselling book, THE NATURAL INSOMNIA SOLUTION.

4.  **STRESS REMEDIES** – such as meditation, mindful-
    ness, journaling, exercise, yoga, and connecting with
    friends and family. Helping patients heal from any
    kind of stress is the major focus of my work because,
    after nearly two decades in practice as a naturopathic
    doctor, I am convinced it is the biggest factor in our
    overall wellness.

I want to close by assuring you that it *is* possible to recover from depression and neurotransmitter imbalances. However, full recovery can be a long, gradual process, and will
require patience and full commitment to your own
needs. That's what I call being a Stress Warrior.

Many of us have been taught to put ourselves last in life,
and are not used to making ourselves our top priority, so
even this can shift in mindset can be a challenge. The road
back to health can also entail a significant learning curve, as
you reeducate yourself on how food, nutrients, and stress impact your health.

But I also want to assure you that you don't need to walk
this path alone – nor should you. You will need friends, family, and at least one experienced and trusted practitioner to
support you as you create change in your life. NEVER stop
your prescription medication without the guidance of your
health professional. Get all the care and support you need as
you go through this process.

You might not feel it now, but: **You are worth it.**

Most of my patients who have suffered from depression tell me the journey back from it is a profound experience – one where they learned many wonderful things about themselves along the way. I sure did when balancing my neurotransmitters and optimizing my health. My best wishes to you on your journey.

# CHAPTER 10

# Meeting with a Stress Warrior

Dr. Doni:   A Stress Warrior makes choices to be healthy while stressed, and I think, that's what you've been up to.

Andrew:   It's part of it, for sure. Managing stress is part of being healthy. I totally believe that. With running a company, I mean, it's hard. There's stress. Every moment, there's stress.

Dr. Doni:   When you decide to run your own company, you're basically saying, "Okay, I'm signing up for stress here."

Andrew:   Somebody asked me what I did for a living and I said I deal with clients with triple A personalities who are under extreme stress.

Dr. Doni:   Tell me more…

Andrew:   That's truly how it is… dealing with intelligent people that have this super job to do and we're in their way. Or, they want what they want when they want it. We work for the entertainment industry in New York City, and there's a lot of planning behind that. We're an architectural engineering firm that helps with the planning. We're part of a team.

Dr. Doni: Wow.

Andrew: One of the byproducts of what we do is that we get them the permits to do their thing. If they don't get the permits, they can't go any further.

Dr. Doni: I see. Basically, not only are you saying, "Okay, I'm going to run my own business," which is a stress in itself, but you're dealing with an industry that is inherently stressful.

Andrew: Yeah, it's stressful.

Dr. Doni: Okay, you definitely have to be a stress warrior then. I know that over the past few years, you've done a lot stress recovery and I want to hear more about what difference you've noticed.

Andrew: One of the things that I've learned to do is ... There's a whole bunch of things but one is to stop saying yes to everything. You have to know when to say no. That's one thing. Another thing is to trust other people to do their job. You can't do everything. You can't even try to do everything. You have to trust people to get their job done.

Dr. Doni:    That's awesome. What helped you prioritize that? I imagine that you probably thought, "Wow, if I try to do everything, I'm going to feel a lot worse."

Andrew:    There just wasn't enough hours in a day to do everything. I hard to hire people. It took a few years to figure out. Actually, it's to the point where you can't be greedy. That's it. I either pay in the form of higher stress, or I pay for a salary. I've chosen to pay for the infrastructure that I need in order to deal with the stress.

Dr. Doni:    You've been doing this for how many years?

Andrew:    Since 1992

Dr. Doni:    And it was a few years ago when you came to see me, and we found that your adrenals, thyroid and neurotransmitters were really being affected by years of stress. We also reviewed your genetics and addressed those areas as well.

Andrew:    Yeah, right.

Dr. Doni:    And just figuring out how to get that re-optimized, those hormone levels. If you think about that process of getting the thyroid to the right support and the adrenals to the right support, what difference has that made for you?

Andrew:    My energy came up, my sleep got better, which is really important, I think.

Dr. Doni:   Yes, it certainly is.

Andrew:   But yeah, I used to come home exhausted. Being just too tired to eat. Yeah, so eating doesn't get right, your sleeping's not right. You fall into what I call the hamster wheel, which is bad.

Dr. Doni:   Trying to keep up with your business and all your clients.

Andrew:   Then there's family, friends, and extended family.

Dr. Doni:   I see what you mean, when you just feel like all you're doing every day is just trying to race to keep up with this circle that's turning and you're like ready to fall off. What helped you realize you needed help keeping up with this hamster wheel?

Andrew:   My wife helped me realize it because I think I got fogged in at that point. When you're on the hamster wheel, you're fogged in. You only get to think about what's needs to be done or what hasn't been done. You're not thinking outside the box, which is really your internal health.

Dr. Doni:   What I really noticed is you were very consistent with implementing everything I suggested. What effect do you think that has had?

Andrew:   Well, I think I have the energy to keep up. The energy to keep up is a really big thing, right?

Dr. Doni:   That's huge. Because you gotta keep going because people are relying on you.

Andrew:     Yeah, and that's where the stress comes from. Being too responsible. I admire people who are less responsible. They're really happy.

Dr. Doni:   That's a good point. You're like, "What would it be like to be not so responsible?" But at least, if you're going to be so responsible, being able to stay ahead. Have enough energy to handle those responsibilities. But it sounds like a relief, like, "At least I know what to do to keep up."

Andrew:     Right. I think we realize that what we do is not life and death situations. It's not like someone's going to get hurt. 99% of the things work themselves out, if you allow them to.

Dr. Doni:   That's amazing. Do you think something about helping your body recover from stress helped you have those kind of realizations?

Andrew:     Yeah, my mental clarity improved. It all comes down to sleep, you know. I want to wake refreshed, not tired.

Dr. Doni:   And you can see things more clearly.

Andrew:     I see things a lot clearer. That was really helpful.

Dr. Doni:   That is pretty amazing. In my notes, I was thinking of your experience of the stress shifted. Instead of feeling in the stress...

Andrew: Yes, now I feel as though I'm sitting outside the stress. Yeah, I'm able to see the cause of the stress and with the identification of it, then I can deal with it. And not even me, but the people around me too. It's how I act, kind of comes down the pyramid, the stress pyramid. So, who's on the top of that pyramid and once that's diffused, it seems to trickle down.

Dr. Doni: That's amazing. So it ends up ... your whole team can be more successful or efficient when you're efficient.

Andrew: It's little things, like my employee may text "I'm late for work, my train is stuck." I'll text back, "Okay, thanks for telling me. Enjoy your time on the stuck train. But it's okay. Don't stress. It will all work out."

Dr. Doni: That's so awesome. So you talk about stress? I think for a lot of people it's this elephant in the room, but they might not be mentioning it. But, you're saying, just mention the elephant in the room.

Andrew: Yes, and I do it with clients too, when we do the schedule, or budget, or when we do the project planning...I say "Alright, now this is what the stress is going to be and how we are going to approach it." I think they appreciate it.

Dr. Doni: I would think so because like with anything, when you're aware of it, you can make a plan around it.

Andrew: Exactly.

Dr. Doni: That's so awesome. It's so helpful.

Andrew: I think it comes from, you know, getting your health back in line, which again, is the fog. It's being in the fog, being on that hamster wheel, not getting sleep, not eating right, feeling run down. I used to come home gray and I was like, "I gotta sit down."

Dr. Doni: I think too, if I remember correctly, there'd be times when you'd be more likely to go for some alcohol to deal with the stress.

Andrew: Yes, and now I have really stopped alcohol intake. It was 2012 is when I started my new regimen with your help.

Dr. Doni: 2012, okay. So that's like six years.

Andrew: Six years.

Dr. Doni: Amazing. And it was finding how can you ... what things can you put in place to help you stay ahead of the stress so that you're not in that position of feeling like alcohol is the only way to numb it for a minute.

Andrew:     Right, so with some lifestyle changes, absolutely. Or vice changes, I guess.

Dr. Doni:   Yeah, but it's really common. I think a lot of people turn to alcohol for stress management.

Andrew:     My son, he's 21 years old and he was not sleeping. He had severe insomnia. He went to a doctor and the doctor said, "Write down your schedule." When you eat, when you sleep, what your activities are. My son did it, and noticed the effect drinking alcohol was having on him. It was disrupting his sleep. So he quit drinking. I'm really proud of him actually.

Dr. Doni:   It really is something.

Andrew:     I told him he's 40 years ahead of me.

Dr. Doni:   Imagine what else he can do with all that extra time. I think it's because he sees you taking steps to improve your health.

Andrew:     Yeah, could be.

Dr. Doni:   You figured out a way to stay healthy while stressed and be able to then serve people with your business and have more time to enjoy for yourself and your family.

Andrew:     It's a battle. It's a daily battle. It's hard.

Dr. Doni:   Just keeping up with it all.

Andrew: It's easy to fall too.

Dr. Doni: I see. So, do you feel you always need to be aware?

Andrew: Yes, It's a narrow path. Have you heard of the straight and narrow? That's what it is.

Dr. Doni: Like walking a tightrope? Do you feel like you're more aware of if you are just a little too close to the edge, and then you know how to correct?

Andrew: Yes, there are ways to correct. Either it's a phone call or whatever. As soon as you can identify the stress, you have the broadcast it to the powers that be, pretty much.

Dr. Doni: And get a shift to happen so that things get back, because you know if not then it's just going to spiral, is what I'm hearing from you.

Andrew: It also helps that I've been practicing Tai Chi for 20 years now and that's really helpful. It's only like eight minutes a day.

Dr. Doni: Eight minutes?

Andrew: Eight to ten minutes a day in the morning and that's it. But I think it's a grounding form of meditation actually. I think that's been helpful, yeah. The days I don't do it, about four o'clock in the afternoon I feel a little bit on the tired side and my body aches. I would feel it physically that I didn't do it. Also mentally.

Dr. Doni:   It's like your meditation; you're stress reducer and you have it in a schedule, so it's every day.

Andrew:   Every morning, when I wake up, it's the first thing I do.

Dr. Doni:   Is there anything you think of that you do that makes a difference?

Andrew:   Weekly, for the past year now, I joined a gym. I try to go twice a week. I want to go more, but I try not to get stressed out about it. I'm not talking about doing some super-duper workout. It's like 40 minutes and the prize at the end is you get to take a steam shower and shave. It's a little bit of pampering there at the end, you earned it.

Dr. Doni:   That's awesome. So it is a stress reduction in that way too. And plus you've made a lot of diet changes too, over the past several years, based on your food sensitivity results and in order to bring your blood sugar levels down.

Andrew:   Yeah.

Dr. Doni:   Does it get hard to stay with that or you just feel like it's part of your stress plan and you stay with it.

Andrew:   Sometimes I cheat. I can, because I'm going to the gym. I actually used to weight myself every-day, but now it's like twice a week. So I'll see it if I start getting above a certain weight and then I'll go back on track.

Dr. Doni:    Did you lose weight over that time?

Andrew:     Yeah, 2012 I was like 195. Now I'm at 162, so 30 pounds.

Dr. Doni:    30 pounds. That's significant.

Andrew:     Yeah, I lost 30 pounds.

Dr. Doni:    30 pounds. Better energy, better sleep, better mental clarity – that's amazing.

Andrew:     It's funny, those 30 pounds. I stopped drinking martinis, I stopped drinking beer, stopped eating pizza and stopped eating pasta and breads. So, those five basically, just dropped those five items from my diet and the pounds just melted off me, pretty much melted off me.

Dr. Doni:    That's amazing.

Andrew:     And that's also when I started working with you to get my thyroid right and you suggested supplements and herbs to help with adrenal recovery and neurotransmitters as well. Now it's maintenance really. Just keeping it up.

Dr. Doni:    Wow, awesome. I'm so excited for you. I really am.

Andrew:     I try. I do fall of the wagon here and there, but I don't stress out about it.

Dr. Doni:    You don't stress about falling off the wagon. Because that's not going to help any way.

Andrew:    Exactly. That's not going to help any way.

Dr. Doni:   It's like, "Okay." That's just part of it. It's almost like anticipating that and keep going." And you know what being "on" is, so you know what to come back to. That's awesome.

Andrew:    I think the biggest thing is, I think to myself "is this a life or death situation?"

Dr. Doni:   Is it really worth the stress?

Andrew:    Yeah. What level of stress should this really be?

Dr. Doni:   So, you're choosing, really choosing, how you respond in each moment.

Andrew:    And what to stress about or be concerned about. I think you can often shift stress down to "concern." It's like what am I concerned about today. What are my concerns today? As opposed to what I'm stressing about today.

Dr. Doni:   And even just that mindset shift helps.

Andrew:    It helps absolutely.

Dr. Doni:   That's awesome. Thank you for sharing. And keep going!

Andrew:    I will, I'll try. I see so many of my friends at the same age as me who are struggling with their health now and taking lots of prescription medications. I'm just so grateful for your help and all you helped me to implement the past few years. It has changed my life.

# CHAPTER 11

# Integrate Self CARE

Our goal is to be resilient NOT invincible.

It often seems that we "should" be invincible. Superheroes and supermoms getting everything done in a flash. Invincible to stress and not needing sleep or self-care. But hey, I think we are starting to find that to be an unattainable illusion. We are susceptible to stress. We are not robots. We are human. And humans are not invincible.

We have to choose a different approach. A different mindset. Resilience is what can help us succeed under stress. The ability to bounce back, recover, persevere. And to be resilient to stress, we must first give ourselves self-care.

We need breaks, rest, sleep, food, water, love and connection. As soon as we ignore those needs, our bodies will start showing signs of stress. That's when symptoms and conditions develop. And when we give our bodies what they need - we recover.

It's a balance. A moving, shifting process. A practice. The practice of being human. Of being a Stress Warrior. You can do it too. I know you can. First stop trying to be invincible. Give that up. Make a 180 and start down the path of resilience starting with self-care.

To help get you started, I created a plan using the word "care" to remind us of the activities we can choose daily to build resilience to stress. You can start these CARE activities right away. Allow them to become second nature. Part of your life and usual routine. In this way, they will not only help you to recover from stress, but to be more resilient to whatever stress comes along.

If you'd like to read all the research behind these activities and why I chose them, please refer to my books: The Stress Remedy and Stress Remedies. In those books I go into great detail connecting the dots between diet, sleep, stress reducing activities, and exercise, and how they help us in many ways. In this chapter, my goal is to help you understand what is included in each activity so you can start getting the benefits of self CARE.

## Self CARE activities:

**Clean Eating** involves figuring out which foods are stressful to your body and then avoiding them. Foods that *increase* stress in our bodies include sugar, high fructose corn syrup, farmed fish, and hormone-filled dairy products. Highly processed foods or fast food also put a lot of additional stress on the body. Foods that are triggering inflammation in your body due to leaky gut and antibody responses are also increasing stress.

Instead, try to stick to fresh vegetables, fruits, nuts, seeds and even fish, poultry, and meats – and choose organic whenever you can. But don't eat too much at one time. Keep in mind that whatever you eat at one sitting has to be digested right then – and if you eat too much, you are likely to experience digestive upset such as reflux, bloating, and gas. The exact 'right amount' varies from person to person so there will be some trial and error to find what works best for you.

The aim is to feel "not hungry" and remember, it takes 20 minutes for your brain to know that you ate so don't keep eating until you feel full. Instead, start with a small serving (say the amount that would fit in a small bowl or plate) and then wait and see how you feel. If you feel too full, then eat less the next time. If you feel hungry again in an hour, then try eating a slightly larger portion next time.

Eat to Balance Your Blood Sugar Levels. All of us, not just those with diabetes, need to be thinking of our blood sugar levels because fluctuations in blood sugar is known to put stress on the body. To do that, try to decrease the amount of sugar and carbs you eat overall and space your meals regularly through the day.

How often to eat varies from person to person – someone whose blood sugar levels tend to drop low may need to eat a small amount of food every 2 hours or so. Otherwise, I recommend eating about every 3 to 4 hours through the day, and don't eat within 2 to 3 hours of bedtime.

By making some simple changes to your diet you'll also be healing leaky gut, balancing the healthy bacteria in your digestion, and decreasing inflammation.

**Adequate Sleep** allows our bodies a chance to rest and recover. Even while we sleep, our bodies are responding to our environment, including the darkness, sounds, temperature, electromagnetics, and more. By providing a clean and sleep supportive, you'll sleep better and be healthier. In fact, lack of sleep is one of the biggest potential stressors for our bodies. That's why I wrote a bestselling book about natural ways to improve your sleep.

We need at least 7.5 to 9 hours of sleep each night. That requires that we stick to a regular bedtime, and take steps to prevent various factors from disrupting our sleep. Light exposure at night, for example, is one of the most common disruptions considering that we are so often exposed to lights and devices. Light (and blue-light in particular) inhibits melatonin, which is our sleep hormone. Without enough melatonin, we are likely to have a much harder time staying asleep.

The effects of stress, including cortisol going up in the evening (instead of down) and calming neurotransmitters become depleted, also disrupt sleep. This means that stress recovery will likely improve your sleep. And once you are sleeping better, it is sleep that will help you stay resilient to stress. See Resources of this book for more help with sleep.

**Reduce Stress** with what I refer to as "Stress Remedies," which are activities that have been found by research to decrease the feeling of being stressed as well as to help optimize hormones and neurotransmitters associated with stress. They include everything from laughing, listening to music, gardening, calling a friend, and drinking a cup of tea to practicing meditation and taking your dog for a walk.

I wrote all about them and the research that supports the concept in my bestselling book, STRESS REMEDIES.

At first, it may be hard to imagine these activities can make that much of a difference or how you can possibly find the time to incorporate them into your day, but I'm here to say they *do* make a difference – so it is worth making time in your schedule to implement them even and especially amidst a storm of stress. I know this not just based on the research, but from trying them out for myself, too.

Spending time in nature is arguably one of the best stress remedies there is. It can benefit your health even with relatively short durations of exposure. Spending time looking at a computer screen, on the other hand, increases health risks and mortality. Perhaps it is time for a dose of nature? Even bringing nature indoors by having a house plant has been shown to make a substantial difference to one's health.

Pet therapy, or animal-assisted therapy as it is called in research, was first studied in the 1960s by Dr. Boris Levinson, a child psychologist who found that having his dog in sessions helped his patients. However, it is also said that Florence Nightingale and Sigmund Freud found much earlier that pets helped in their care of patients.

119

Research into pet therapy for both adults and children has surged in recent years and has found that animals help humans to decrease pain, anxiety, depression, and fatigue. Studies of animals in nursing homes show a decrease in loneliness and having a pet is known to decrease heart disease risk, increase survival after a heart attack, and decrease the need for medical intervention after stressful life events. The evidence overall indicates that, just as animals respond to people's attention, they equally have a calming influence on us that can help our healing.

For this reason, I started a not-for-profit organization for cat rescue and care on Long Island, New York. My companies, including Nature Empowered Nutritionals, contributes 20% of proceeds to Cat Care because I believe helping animals and humans to support each other is essential for our wellness.

Another effective way you can reduce stress is with an activity that has been used for centuries – meditation. I first learned about meditation 20 years ago when I was a naturopathic medical student. Since then, and as I continued to research stress, I have read study after study indicating the benefits of meditation including: improved mood; decreased anxiety; better sleep; decreased risk of heart attack; and perhaps most exciting, nerve healing (which was previously thought to be not possible in adults), resulting in higher IQ and creativity.

A couple years ago I decided to participate in an 8-week Mindfulness Based Stress Reduction (MBSR) course, as developed by Jon Kabat-Zinn at the University of Massachusetts

Medical School in 1979, which I highly recommend. There are also many meditation courses available now, including some online programs (see Resources section of this book).

Mindfulness is actually a type of meditation. Jon Kabat-Zinn says that, "Mindfulness means paying attention in a particular way; on purpose, in the present moment, and non-judgmentally."

Meditation in various forms, including transcendental meditation, induces a type of brain activity that is different than being alert or being asleep. It is actually 2 to 5 times more relaxing and restful than sleep and it is this deep state of relaxation which allows the body to heal from stress and, because it involves both sides of your brain, it helps build the communication pathways between the logical left brain and the creative right brain.

## How Do Mindfulness and Meditation Work?

Both meditation and mindfulness allow your brain to reconcile everything that's going on in your life and help bring your focus to the present moment. All of this helps you better connect with your intuition and stay out of a state of stress, even when you are not meditating.

They both also:

- Decrease cortisol – your stress hormone
- Increase serotonin and dopamine levels – the neurotransmitters that influence mood, sleep and focus

- Increase function of the prefrontal cortex of the brain, helping you organize and respond without being in a state of fear

- Positively influence growth factors and telomeres, which protect your genes (HERE IS AN ARTICLE I WROTE ABOUT TELOMERES if you want to learn more about this).

By focusing your mind in a certain way, you can actually change your brain, your hormones and the way your genes influence your health – powerful stuff!

## How to Start Meditating or Practicing Mindfulness

Meditation is often represented as sitting still, cross-legged on the floor, with your eyes closed. That is certainly one way to meditate, but it is also possible to meditate or practice mindfulness while sitting in a chair or doing activities such as walking, doing the dishes, brushing your teeth, eating, or showering.

Another form of mindfulness is biofeedback, which involves focusing your attention on your body to change your blood pressure or heart-rate variability. Personally, I like to practice mindfulness while taking care of our rescue cats and while taking our dog, Aphrodite, for a walk

A simple way to get started is to put your focus on just one thing. For example, you could put all your focus on the word "one." Or you could put your focus on your breath – inhale slowly, exhale slowly, and repeat, noticing how each breath feels. Or you could focus on a "mantra" – a positive affirmation or thought, similar to a prayer.

Whatever you choose to focus on, each time you notice that your mind has wandered to another thought (and it will), quietly and calmly bring your attention back to that one thing. You could spend as little as 5 minutes or as long as an hour, or even several hours, practicing mindfulness.

During my MBSR class we started by eating a raisin in a mindful way. We first picked up the raisin and looked at it. Then we felt it and smelled it. Finally, we put the raisin in our mouth, at first not biting into it, and then noticing how it tastes when we did bite into it. We chewed it at least ten times before swallowing it. A raisin never tasted so good! You could try this (as long as you are okay eating a raisin) as a way to start experiencing mindfulness.

## Using Meditation to Decrease Stress

The more you practice, the easier it will become to integrate meditation and mindfulness into your daily life. The more you can do this, the better your body will be able to withstand stress, increasing your resilience and reducing the negative effects of stress on your health. Not only that, but you'll also sleep better, allowing your body to heal even more. Studies show that even just 1 hour of meditation a week for 12 weeks will reduce stress and improve sleep.

Here are a few of my **favorite resources**, including some recommended by my patients – try them out and see how you feel:

- ZivaMeditation: online training program with my friend Emily Fletcher
- INSIGHTTIMER.COM: offering guided meditations, as well as timers and sounds
- ZIVAMEDITATION.COM: offering online and in person meditation training
- HEADSPACE.COM: an online tool and app to help you meditate
- MINDVALLEYACADEMY.COM: offering courses on mindfulness and more
- HEARTMATH.ORG: a website offering support to implement mindfulness
- *HAPPINESS THROUGH MEDITATION*: a book by my friend and colleague, Dr. Paul Epstein

We are all exposed to stress, now probably more than ever before, so the key to staying well is to do things that help your body recover from stress better.

Stress is also caused by exposure to the toxins in personal care products that we apply to our bodies daily. This is such a large, but often unrecognized stress to the body, which is why decreasing exposure to those stressful chemicals is an important part of the CARE plan

Although these substances are invisible and are used on the *outside* of our bodies, research is showing that they can wreak havoc on our **insides;** and not just in the next few days or weeks, but for years to come. That's because anything you put on your skin can be absorbed into your body – into your fat tissue and into your blood stream. Just because you put it on the outside doesn't mean it won't get inside and cause trouble there too!

There are a number of ways that the ingredients in our beauty and skincare products cause stress to our bodies and potentially damage our health. One of the first ways chemicals cause trouble is by disrupting hormone levels. These chemicals look similar to the hormones produced in our bodies and are referred to as "endocrine disruptors" because they can prevent the production or inhibit the action of the hormones that are normally made in our bodies (thyroid hormone, insulin, estrogen, progesterone, testosterone and others).

Some of the common places you may be exposed to these chemical toxins and others are:

- Shampoo and conditioner
- Lotions
- Toothpaste

- Soap
- Facial cleansers and masks
- Make up
- Nail polish
- Deodorant
- Sunscreen
- Mouthwash

**These are my favorite resources for toxin-free, stress-free products:**

- SKIN DEEP AT THE ENVIRONMENTAL WORKING GROUP is a very useful online resource that allows you to search for cosmetic products and tells you whether they are of low, medium or high toxic hazard.

- A company called **Made Safe** has created a certification process for products that are toxin-free, GO TO THEIR WEBSITE to see a list of their certified products.

- CINCOVIDAS is an informational website developed by my patient, Britta Aragon, who created a line of toxin-free skincare products called CVskinlabs. I'm very proud of Britta who was inspired to create these products after being treated for cancer.

- My friend and colleague, Dr. Trevor Cates is THESPADR. She has designed a skincare line that is completely free of toxins.

126

- CRUELTYFREEKITTY is a website recommended by my daughter, Ella, where you can search for products to find out if they do animal testing. I find that companies that don't test on animals also tend to stay away from using chemicals.

**Exercise and Movement** – whether strength training, cardio, or any other kind of exercise that appeals to you – has consistently been shown to help us recover from stress. Exercising in some way, each day, even for a small amount of time, makes a big difference in preventing various forms of chronic disease.

When you can combine exercise with being out in nature (by going for a hike, skiing, or swimming for example) you've effectively combined nature with exercise for cumulative benefit to your health.

What might be surprising to some is that even small amounts each day can make a huge difference. You don't have to push yourself to your limit in a spin class or run a marathon to realize the benefits of exercise. Just a short walk each day can help. And what I like is that it counts as a form of mindfulness too.

Exercise can be "me time," a place to sort out your thoughts and better prioritize the day's tasks.

Here are some of the good things that happens with moderate exercise:

- You get a boost of immune function and healthy detoxification to fight off viruses

- Increased insulin function helps manage elevated blood sugar

- Increases growth hormone to build muscles and increased energy endurance during the daytime

- It boosts your Basal Metabolic Rate so you can burn calories more efficiently – even when you are not working out

- Exercise aids in sleep quality, which is ELEMENTAL to help your body repair itself from stress

- It reduces risk of cancer, heart disease, diabetes and memory loss

- It has been shown to improve and increase libido

- And it creates community with others who exercise

Again, don't be hard on yourself here! Start with small amounts, including core strength. Then gradually increase it based on how you feel as your adrenal glands start to recover.

It can feel weird at first to do something different. That's because it is not the "usual" pattern. But soon, as you engage in more supportive activities – even starting with 2 minutes each day – it will be come your norm. You'll push out the "hard on yourself" mentality little by little as you make progress. Go at your own pace. Give it a try and let me know what you notice!

For a free 7-day video series from me to help you with implementing CARE, go to DoctorDoni.com/stress-reset.

I'm so excited for you to implement everything you've learned in this book, in a way that matches for your body, your genetics and your stress exposure. I encourage you to work with a naturopathic doctor or other practitioner who has completed training with me, so you are sure to get the best results. I know what is possible, and I want that for you.

Thank you for joining me on this path to learning to be a Stress Warrior. I welcome you to check out the resources and support programs described in the final pages of the book. And please, reach out, let me know how this information helps you, and share it with your loved ones who may also be seeking support to be healthy even though we live in a world filled with potential stress.

You now have the information and tools to be a resilient Stress Warrior.

- - - - - - - - - - - - - - - - - - - - - - - - - - - - - - - - - - - - - - - - - - -

## TAKE AWAY NOTES:

CARE stands for: C_____A_____R_____E_____

CARE activities I'd like to try: _____

- - - - - - - - - - - - - - - - - - - - - - - - - - - - - - - - - - - - - - - - - - -

# Resources, Products and Programs

## Tests, Health Panels, Supplements and Where to Get Them

The following tests and supplements are all offered by Dr. Doni. If they are available via her online store, you will find the links to them below. Alternatively, you can search for them by name by going to Dr. Doni's online store at DrDoni-Store.com.

To review the services Dr. Doni offers, including her Stress Warrior Online Course, Adrenal Recovery Consultation Package and her High Performer Acceleration Program, as well as her other group and online programs, visit https://doctordoni.com/work-with-dr-doni/. From there you'll be able to apply to work with her one-on-one or with one of her associates.

# Tests and Health Panels

### Blood work

The blood work mentioned in this book can be ordered directly and paid out of pocket (not billed to insurance) at YourLabWork.com and/or UltaLabs.

### IgG and IgA Food Panel

An IgG and IgA food panel can help you determine whether or not you have delayed food sensitivities, and which foods you might be sensitive to. Done with a finger-prick blood sample, you can do this test at home and send it to the laboratory through the mail. The lab with check your sample against 96 of the most common foods, including gluten and dairy, to find out if your immune system is attacking the food you are eating. You can order this test through your naturopathic doctor or from Dr. Doni at:

- IgG and IgA Food Sensitivity Home Testing
  https://www.drdonistore.com/ gG-IgA-Food-Sensitivity-Home-Testing_p_262.html

### Estrogen, progesterone and testosterone levels

While these hormones can be measured in blood, saliva or urine, Dr. Doni's preference at this point in time, and for the purpose of understanding the hormone levels and metabolism, is the dried urine test from Precision Analytical (DUTCH test). This panel is able to show how much estrogen and progesterone is being metabolized and how well estrogen is being metabolized. The dried urine test is also an effective way to evaluate estrogen and progesterone levels even when taking hormones. A practitioner with training in the use of these tests will be able to tell you if testing is right for you and, if so, which test will be most helpful. Ask your naturopathic doctor or Dr. Doni about arranging to do this test.

### Cortisol, DHEA, and melatonin

A saliva or urine panel can be used to measure cortisol, DHEA, and melatonin. Precision Analytical can run these hormones along with estrogen, progesterone and testosterone as described above. For cortisol, it is best to collect four timed samples, which are usually collected upon waking, mid-day, evening, bedtime. In cases where you are waking in the middle of the night, collecting a saliva or urine sample at that time can be helpful as well. Melatonin is most often measured at 10 pm when it should be at the highest level. In some cases it will also be measured in the night upon waking and/or other times of day, especially if you work the night shift.

If you are interested in these tests, ask your naturopathic doctor or contact Dr. Doni's office at DrDoni.com.

### Neurotransmitter levels

Urine can be used to measure adrenaline levels as well as neurotransmitters such as serotonin, GABA, glutamate, dopamine, norepinephrine and epinephrine. In most cases the second morning urine is collected. If you are waking in the night, a urine sample at the time of waking can be useful. At this time, Dr. Doni recommends Sanesco NeuroLab.

A practitioner with training in the use of these panels will be able to tell you if testing is right for you and, if so, which test will be most helpful. Ask your naturopathic doctor or Dr. Doni's office to arrange this type of panel.

### PCR Specialty Stool Panel

There are several available that Dr. Doni considers to be accurate and useful: GI MAP, Vibrant Gut Zoomer and Genova GI Effects. These panels will all assess for commensal and pathogenic bacteria, parasites and protozoa, and yeast. Additional options are to check for zonulin levels, secretory IgA and inflammatory markers, as well as ability to digest foods and fat. You'll want to work with a practitioner to help you interpret and act on the results.

### Organic Acids, Oxidative Stress, Toxins and Mold Toxins

Great Plains Lab is Dr. Doni's preferred lab for checking organic acids and toxin panels. These are urine tests that provide information about imbalanced gut bacteria, mitochondrial function, nutrient levels, and other metabolites that influence sleep. Evaluating for toxins is an important consideration when it comes to insomnia and other health issues.

### Genetic Panel

There are several genetic panels to choose from that check common gene SNPS, such as MTHFR.

Toolbox Genomics Ancestry.com combined with Strate-Gene

**NOTE:** If you are interested in meeting with Dr. Doni to have her help with any of these tests, you can learn about her services at DrDoni.com. Then, once the results come in, you'll be able to consult with her to discuss your results. She can also advise you on dietary changes and suggest supplements that may help.

## Protein Shakes and Supplements

### Protein Shakes

- **Dr. Doni's Pea Protein, comes in Chocolate, Vanilla, Berry.** It contains 16 grams of protein per scoop plus nutrients, including methylfolate, and is sweetened with stevia.

https://www.drdonistore.com/Dr-Donis-Pea-Protein-Shake_p_733.html

- **Samples of Dr. Doni's Pea Protein** are available for free (with the cost of shipping), so you can try it out and see if you like it.

https://www.drdonistore.com/Dr-Donis-Pea-Protein-Shake-Samples_p_792.html

- **Plain Organic Pea Protein** is a very good option for those who have more severe leaky gut and need to keep things simple, and for those who prefer protein powder without stevia.

https://www.drdonistore.com/Organic-PurePea-Protein-UnflavoredUnsweetened-450-g_p_864.html

- **Innate Vegan Protein** is pea protein with vanilla, cinnamon and stevia.

https://www.drdonistore.com/Vegan-Protein-Vanilla-169-oz_p_550.html

- **Vital Proteins Collagen** comes in marine and beef versions and contains 11 grams of protein in 2 scoops.

https://www.drdonistore.com/Collagen-Peptides-10-oz_p_780.html

- **DFH Chocolate Collagen contains** beef collagen, with cocoa, stevia.

https://www.drdonistore.com/PurePaleo-Protein-Chocolate-810-grams_p_914.html

## Balance Blood Sugar and Optimize Insulin Function

- **Metabolic Xtra** contains chromium and berberine, two substances known to support insulin function and stabilize blood sugar levels.

https://www.drdonistore.com/Metabolic-Xtra-90-capsules_p_263.html

- Cinnamon and other herbs and nutrients that help with blood sugar regulation can be found in combination products, such as **Blood Sugar Support.**

https://www.drdonistore.com/Blood-Sugar-Support-120-Vegetarian-Capsules_p_498.html

## Increase GABA

- One option is to take actual GABA, such as in **Calming Support by Dr. Doni:**

https://www.drdonistore.com/Dr-Donis-Calming-Support-90-capsules_p_980.html

- 4-amino-3-phenylbutyric acid is a precursor nutrient to GABA and is used to increase the production of GABA. Example product is **Kavinace:**

https://www.drdonistore.com/Kavinace_p_424.html

- Combining phenyl-butyric acid, melatonin and 5-HTP (the precursor to serotonin) is indicated when GABA, serotonin and melatonin all need support. If your naturopathic doctor determines that you could use serotonin and melatonin support, you might consider **Kavinace Ultra:**

https://www.drdonistore.com/Kavinace-Ultra-PM-30-capsules_p_212.html

- **Dr. Doni's Sleep Support** contains GABA, L-Theanine, along with melatonin, 5HTP (serotonin support), vitamin B6 and several calming herbs, including Passion Flower, Lemon Balm, Chamomile and Valerian.

https://www.drdonistore.com/Dr-Donis-Sleep-Support-60-capsules_p_979.html

### Increase Serotonin

- 5-HTP is the precursor nutrient to serotonin. Example products are **Serene:** https://www.drdonistore.com/Serene-60-capsules_p_384.html and **5HTP by Prothera:**

https://www.drdonistore.com/5-HTP-100-mg-100-capsules_p_773.html

- Nutrients to support the production of serotonin include vitamin B6, B12, folate, zinc and 5HTP. An example product is **TravaCor**:

https://www.drdonistore.com/Travacor_p_456.html

- Tryptophan is a precursor to serotonin. It is first converted to 5HTP then to serotonin. An example product is:

https://www.drdonistore.com/L-Tryptophan-60-capsules_p_585.html

- **Dr. Doni's Sleep Support** contains GABA, L-Theanine, along with melatonin, 5HTP (serotonin support), vitamin B6 and several calming herbs, including Passion Flower, Lemon Balm, Chamomile and Valerian.

https://www.drdonistore.com/Dr-Donis-Sleep-Support-60-capsules_p_979.html

### Decrease Glutamate

- L-theanine, CoQ10 and N-AcetylCysteine all help to decrease glutamate when it is too high. An example product containing all three is **Calm G**:

https://www.drdonistore.com/Calm-G-90-capsules_p_217.html

- **Dr. Doni's Sleep Support** contains GABA (which counterbalances GABA), L-Theanine, along with melatonin, 5HTP (serotonin support), vitamin B6 and several calming herbs, including Passion Flower, Lemon Balm, Chamomile and Valerian.

https://www.drdonistore.com/Dr-Donis-Sleep-Support-60-capsules_p_979.html

## Decrease Cortisol

- Phosphatidylserine is a nutrient known to help get the brain out of stress mode and decrease cortisol. An example product is PS Plus:

https://www.drdonistore.com/PS-Plus-60-capsules_p_1055.html

- Banaba leaf and phosphatidylserine work in combination to help decrease cortisol when it is too high. An example product is **Calm CP**:

https://www.drdonistore.com/Calm-CP-60-capsules_p_215.html

- Ashwagandha root and phosphatidylserine all help to decrease cortisol. An example product is **Stress Support:**

https://www.drdonistore.com/Dr-Donis-Stress-Support-90-capsules_p_981.html

- Magnolia bark and Ziziphus are also known to decrease cortisol levels that are too high. **Seditol** contains these two herbs:

https://www.drdonistore.com/Seditol-60-capsules_p_761.html

## Decrease Norepinephrine (aka adrenaline)

- Magnesium and vitamin B6 help process norepinephrine to epinephrine, essentially decreasing adrenaline levels. An example is **Magnesium Plus**:

https://www.drdonistore.com/Magnesium-Plus-100-vegetarian-capsules_p_35.html

- **Stress Support by Dr. Doni** contains B6 and magnesium to decrease adrenaline, along with ingredients to decrease cortisol, and calming herbs:

https://www.drdonistore.com/Dr-Donis-Stress-Support-90-capsules_p_981.html

- High concentrations of the herb rhodiola helps to decrease cortisol and adrenaline levels. One example of a supplement containing a high concentration of rhodiola is Calm PRT:

https://www.drdonistore.com/Calm-PRT_p_428.html

### Calm nervous system (overall)

Herbs that are calming to the nervous system include valerian, chamomile, passionflower, hops and California poppy.

- One example product is **Sweet Dreams** herbal tincture:

https://www.drdonistore.com/Sweet-Dreams-2-oz_p_419.html

- **Dr. Doni's Sleep Support** contains GABA, L-Theanine, along with melatonin, 5HTP (serotonin support), vitamin B6 and several calming herbs, including Passion Flower, Lemon Balm, Chamomile and Valerian.

https://www.drdonistore.com/Dr-Donis-Sleep-Support-60-capsules_p_979.html

- **Hemp oil contains cannabinoids** which have been shown to help calming the nervous system and with stress recovery in general. Here are two example products: Hemp oil that is organic and $CO_2$ extracted: https://www.drdonistore.com/Hemp-Oil-30-capsules_p_1061.html and CannabOmega (with fish oil):

https://www.drdonistore.com/CannabOmega-60-softgels_p_1012.html

Nutrients that calm the nervous system include **magnesium, B6, theanine** and **glycine**.

- Glycine can be found in both **Calm CP** and **Calming Support** (see above), as well as **Sleep Reset™ sachets** (see description under "melatonin" below).

- Magnesium and B6 can be found in **Stress Support by Dr. Doni and in Magnesium Plus.** See above for descriptions of these products.

- Magnesium threonate, which is particularly calming to the nervous system, is found in **NeuroMag**:

https://www.drdonistore.com/NeuroMag-90-vegetarian-capsules_p_896.html

- **Dr. Doni's Sleep Support** contains GABA, L-Theanine, along with melatonin, 5HTP (serotonin support), vitamin B6 and several calming herbs, including Passion Flower, Lemon Balm, Chamomile and Valerian.

https://www.drdonistore.com/Dr-Donis-Sleep-Support-60-capsules_p_979.html

### Sleep Support

Melatonin increases at night when the lights are out and you are sleeping. If you are exposed to light at night, have a low melatonin level, and/or change time zones with travel and need to reset your sleep cycle, you might consider a melatonin supplement. Example products include:

- **Melatonin 3 mg:**

https://www.drdonistore.com/Melatonin-3-mg-60-caps_p_390.html

- **Melatonin-SR 2 mg:**

https://www.drdonistore.com/Melatonin-SR-2-mg-60-capsules_p_417.html

There are also many products that combine melatonin with other sleep support ingredients. Examples of these include:

- **Dr. Doni's Sleep Support** contains GABA, L-Theanine, along with melatonin, 5HTP (serotonin support), vitamin B6 and several calming herbs, including Passion Flower, Lemon Balm, Chamomile and Valerian.

https://www.drdonistore.com/Dr-Donis-Sleep-Support-60-capsules_p_979.html

- **ProThrivers Wellness Sleep** has melatonin with theanine, magnesium, and Magnolia (to lower cortisol):

https://www.drdonistore.com/ProThrivers-Wellness-Sleep_p_463.html

- **Kavinace ULTRA** contains 5HTP, phenylbutyric acid and melatonin:

https://www.drdonistore.com/Kavinace-Ultra-PM-30-capsules_p_212.html

- **Sleep Reset™ sachets** contain melatonin with turmeric (anti-inflammatory), 5HTP (serotonin support), theanine (decreases glutamate), glycine, and vitamin B6:

https://www.drdonistore.com/Sleep-Reset-Orange-Flavor--Restful-Sleep-Blend_p_462.html

### Increase Cortisol

Herbs that support adrenal function and cortisol levels are referred to as "adaptogens." Rhodiola is an adaptogen that functions differently at different doses. Low doses of rhodiola can help increase cortisol when it is too low. There are many products that contain rhodiola in combination with other cortisol balancing nutrients and herbs. Some example products are:

- Dr. Doni's **Adrenal Support**: Contains tyrosine to support adrenaline, plus herbs and nutrients to support adrenal function and cortisol production, such as vitamin C, pantothenic acid, Eleutherococcus and Glycyrrhiza (herbal licorice).

https://www.drdonistore.com/Dr-Donis-Adrenal-Support-90-capsules_p_978.html

- **Adrenal Response**: A combination of vitamin C, pantothenate, magnesium, ashwagandha, L-serine, rhodiola extract, holy basil (tulsi) leaf, Cordyceps mushroom mycelia, Reishi mushroom, organic astragulus root, Schizandra, and other active ingredients.

- **Adrenal SAP licorice-free:** A combination of vitamins C, B6 and B5, plus magnesium, zinc, ashwagandha, holy basil (tulsi), Panax ginseng, Siberian ginseng, Schizandra, and astralagus.

- **AdreCor:** Contains the B vitamins, plus vitamin C, tyrosine, and herbs such as Rhodiola and green tea. These have all been shown to restore healthy adrenal function.

https://www.drdonistore.com/AdreCor_p_580.html

- **AdreCor with Licorice:** In addition to the standard AdreCor formula, this product contains licorice extract, which is known to significantly support cortisol levels.

https://www.drdonistore.com/AdreCor-with-Licorice-Root-90-capsules_p_360.html

- **AdreCor with SAMe:** In additional to the standard AdreCor formula, this product contains SAMe, which helps with the conversion from norepinephrine to epinephrine, resulting in healthier adrenaline and energy levels.

https://www.drdonistore.com/AdreCor-with-SAMe-30-capsules_p_361.html

### Increase Norepinephrine (aka adrenaline)

Phenylalanine and tyrosine are precursor nutrients to norepinephrine, so if we need to increase the levels of norepinephrine, we can use those nutrients. Norepinephrine is made in part by the adrenal glands, so we can also increase norepinephrine levels by supporting adrenal gland function using herbs and/or nutrients, such as B vitamins (including pantothenic acid), vitamin C, and eleuthrococcus, glycyrrhiza, and rhodiola. Some suggested products are:

- **Adrenal Support by Dr. Doni:**

https://www.drdonistore.com/Dr-Donis-Adrenal-Support-90-capsules_p_978.html

- **AdreCor** (see description above):

https://www.drdonistore.com/AdreCor_p_580.html

## Liver – Detoxification of Estrogens

- **B vitamins** (B6/P5P, folate/5MTHF and B12) are needed by the liver to detoxify estrogens. An example product is **Methyl-Guard Plus:**

https://www.drdonistore.com/Methyl-Guard-Plus-90-capsules_p_367.html

- **Methylation** is an important step in the detoxification of estrogens. Choline provides methyl groups for that process. An example product is **Optimal PC:**

https://www.drdonistore.com/Optimal-PC-100-Softgels_p_28.html

- **DIM (diindolmethionine)** is a substance from broccoli that supports healthy estrogen metabolism. An example product containing the first and only stable bioavailable form of DIM by DFH:

https://www.drdonistore.com/DIM-Evail_p_666.html

145

- **Sulforaphane glucosinolate (SGS)** is a natural substance derived from the seeds and sprouts of broccoli that is an advanced antioxidant and has chemoprotective properties. An example product is **Crucera-SGS:**

https://www.drdonistore.com/Crucera-SGS-60-vegetarian-capsules_p_413.html

- **DIM with CDG:**

https://www.drdonistore.com/CDG-EstroDIM-60-capsules_p_710.html

- **DIM with CDG and Broccoli:**

https://www.drdonistore.com/DIM-with-Calcium-D-Glucarate-60-capsules_p_965.html

- **Curcumin** has been shown in research to support liver detoxification and decrease inflammation. An example product containing curcumin is **Meriva 500:**

https://www.drdonistore.com/Meriva-500-Soy-Free-120-capsules_p_758.html

- **Milk Thistle (Silymarin)** is supportive of liver detoxification including the production of glutathione. It is also known to assist the body in ridding itself of excess estrogens. Dr. Doni carries a 500-milligram milk thistle supplement at

https://www.drdonistore.com/Milk-Thistle-500-mg-120-veggie-capsules_p_309.html

- **Green Tea Extract (EGCF)** has been shown to help detoxify toxins and estrogens from the body, and decrease the negative effects of excess estrogen. An example product containing highly absorbed green tea is **Green Tea Phytosome:**

https://www.drdonistore.com/Green-Tea-Phytosome-60-capsules_p_350.html

## Estrogen Support

- **Black Cohosh** (Cimicifuga) is an herb that assists with hot flashes, night sweats and other perimenopausal symptoms. It has been shown to be safe for patients who have, or who have had, breast cancer. An example product is **Black Cohosh** by Vitanica:

https://www.drdonistore.com/Black-Cohosh_p_500.html

- **Maca** is an herb that has been researched to help with PMS, perimenopausal and post-menopausal symptoms. It helps balance hormones and supports estrogen levels that are too low. An example product is called **Femmenessence**: For Peri-menopause;

https://www.drdonistore.com/Femmenessence-PRO-PERI-180-vegetarian-capsules_p_53.html For Post-menopause:
https://www.drdonistore.com/Femmenessence-PRO-POST-180-vegetarian-capsules_p_172.html

## Progesterone Support

- **Chaste tree berry (Vitex)** is an herb that supports the ovaries to ovulate and produce hormones on their own. It assists with the communication from the brain to the ovaries, resulting in increased progesterone

147

production by the ovaries. An example product with high effectiveness is **Chaste Tree Berry by Vitanica**:

https://www.drdonistore.com/Chaste-Tree-Berry-60-capsules_p_166.html

- **Wild Yam (Dioscorea villosa)** acts as a mild proges-terone-like substance in the body. It is available in both oral and topical (cream) forms. An example wild yam **cream** is available at

https://www.drdonistore.com/Dioscorea-Cream-56-gms_p_426.html

If you prefer **capsules**, you can find them at

https://www.drdonistore.com/Dioscorea-Capsules-60-vegetarian-capsules_p_427.html

- **Progesterone cream** is derived from plant sources and can be applied topically as a way to support low progesterone levels. One example of a paraben-free cream is **Natural Progeste Cream** at

https://www.drdonistore.com/Natural-Progeste-Cream-35-oz_p_538.html

- **Adrenal support** can support healthy ovarian func-tion and greatly improve perimenopausal and post-menopausal symptoms. One example of such a product is Dr. Doni's Adrenal Support

https://www.drdonistore.com/Dr-Donis-Adrenal-Support-90-capsules_p_978.html

## Decrease Inflammation

Herb that promote a healthy inflammation response in-clude curcumin (from turmeric), skullcap, and rosemary.

Phytocannabinoids from hemp oil (as well as cloves, black pepper, hops and rosemary) are known to decrease inflammation. Omega 3 (fish oils) also decrease inflammation. Bromelain is an enzyme known to decrease inflammation. Example products with these ingredients are:

- **Meriva 500:**

https://www.drdonistore.com/Meriva-500-Soy-Free-120-capsules_p_758.html

- **InflaCalm:**

https://www.drdonistore.com/InflaCalm-SAP-90-capsules_p_807.html

- **Zyflamend:**

https://www.drdonistore.com/Zyflamend-120-Vegetarian-Capsules_p_66.html

- Hemp oil that is organic and CO2 extracted:

https://www.drdonistore.com/Hemp-Oil-30-capsules_p_1061.html

- CannabOmega is hemp oil combined with fish oil:

https://www.drdonistore.com/CannabOmega-60-softgels_p_1012.html

- Omega 3 fish oil in a concentrated form and highest quality, that has been independently tests for metals and toxins is **Ultra Pure Fish Oil:**

https://www.drdonistore.com/Ultra-Pure-Fish-Oil-800-Triglyceride-90-gels_p_44.html

## Leaky Gut Healing Support

- **Leaky Gut Support:**

https://www.drdonistore.com/Dr-Donis-Leaky-Gut-Support-61-oz_p_681.html

149

- ## Enzyme Support:

https://www.drdonistore.com/-Dr-Donis-Enzyme-Support-90-capsules_p_977.html

- ## Probiotic Support:

https://www.drdonistore.com/Dr-Donis-Probiotic-Support-60-vegetarian-capsules_p_271.html

# Recommended Third-Party Products and Resources

**D**r. Doni compiled Stress Warrior supportive products and resources for you here. She does not sell these products or guarantee them. They are listed here because either she or her clients have used them successfully. Find more foods and products Dr. Doni suggests on her Amazon page.

## Gluten-free and Dairy-free Meal Planning and Foods

### PrepDish

No more thinking. No more stress. No more meal time guesswork. With our Gluten Free and Paleo meal plans, you'll enjoy healthy, tasty meals with your family all week long! Receive real-food meal plans via email (you get BOTH gluten free & Paleo plans!). $10 off the premium subscription with code DrDoni.

## PaleoTreats

We've been making foodie-approved Paleo desserts since 2009. We are serious about flavor, texture, ingredients and Paleo. Yes, all of them. We've shipped around the world, from Australia to Afghanistan, and we've ironed out all the kinks of getting a great dessert to your door. Get 10% off with the code DrDoni.

# Organic Mattress

## Samina

Each layer of the system, including the natural mattress, was specifically designed to support something the human body needs while sleeping¬—this is the SAMINA Healthy Sleep Concept. The system works with your body and each layer works synergistically to ensure you fall asleep easy, you stay asleep and reducing or eliminating reasons your bed may cause you to toss and turn or awaken like you're too sweaty, hot or cold, and that you awaken refreshed. From the orthopedic flexible slat frame to the orthopedic pillows, the SAMINA Sleep System contours to each person's individual shape and size.

# Air Filters

Recommended companies that manufacture high-quality air filters:

IQAir

AlenCorp

Austin Air

Air Doctor

## Meditation Online Training

### Ziva Meditation

In only 2 weeks, you can reduce the stress in your body so you can perform at the top of your game. This isn't another challenge, zivaONLINE is a proven, in-depth training that will give you the most powerful meditation practice available. You'll get a powerful combination of: Meditation, mindfulness and manifesting.

## Exercise Online Program

### Flipping 50

Debra shows you how to integrate in fun and easy ways so you can reach your fitness goals.

## Non-Toxic Skincare

### SpaDr

Toxin-free skin care products designed by a naturopathic doctor, Dr. Trevor Cates.

# Stress Warrior Course

## Recover from Stress, Heal Leaky Gut and Optimize Adrenal Function

Start on the path to recovering from stress and becoming resilient to stress, no matter your genetic predispositions. In this online course you'll learn how stress has affected you and what you can do to reverse it. In the process, you'll improve your energy, mood, focus, while getting rid of bloating, extra weight, sleepless nights, as well as aches and pains. Join me in becoming a Stress Warrior!

In this series of online sessions, Dr. Doni will guide you to know how stress has affected your health and the steps to recover. Whether you think you may have adrenal fatigue or adrenal distress, leaky gut or digestive issues... or if you know that you have an MTHFR gene SNP, fatigue, anxiety, or sleep issues... or you simply want to learn how to help your body recover from stress... this course is for you.

## Who Is This Course Fpr?

This course is for anyone who has symptoms associated

with stress exposure. This includes fatigue, insomnia, recurrent infections, digestive issues, rashes, autoimmunity, fertility issues, brain fog, anxiety, depression, pain, headaches, PMS, and/or weight gain. If you think you may have **leaky gut and/or adrenal fatigue** and perhaps also blood sugar and hormone imbalances, this course if for you. It is also for anyone who knows they have an **MTHFR** gene SNP or suspect they may have it and **what to know how to address it.**

This course is particularly great for someone who wants to learn how to understand their own health and results of health panels, and likes to understand the options for supporting your body to heal. Perhaps you'd like to follow this course while also working one-on-one with Dr. Doni (as part of one of her packages) or maybe you prefer to start with this course to learn more on your own.

## What Is MTHFR?

MTHFR is a gene that affects the methylation cycle in the body. When we say someone "has MTHFR", we mean they have a genetic variation of the MTHFR gene, which can cause many health issues. Some women with MTHFR have **miscarriages** or find it **difficult to get pregnant**. Other patients (both men and woman) may suffer from **chronic pain syndrome/fibromyalgia, anxiety, insomnia or depression.** Left unaddressed, having an MTHFR genetic variation can also put you at greater risk for developing serious conditions like **Alzheimer's, heart disease, diabetes or cancer.**

# What Is This Course?

**This is a 6-part online course** (webinar series) with Dr. Doni, where you will learn how stress affects us, how it causes leaky gut and adrenal distress, how to find out if you have leaky gut and adrenal distress, and how to heal your digestion and adrenals, while balancing hormones, neurotransmitters and your immune system. You'll learn what MTHFR is, how it affects your health, how to understand genetic health reports and other health panels related to MTHFR, and how to attain optimal methylation and reclaim your health – naturally.

**Sign up for the Stress Warrior Course here.**

# How Do I Attend The Classes?

There are 6 sessions, each about 60 minutes in length. The classes are delivered online, which means you can attend from anywhere in the world. You will also have access to the video recordings, so you can watch/listen to the class whenever you wish.

# What Will I Learn On The Course?

Over the 6 sessions you will learn:

1. **Effects of Stress.** Fundamentals and science behind stress and HPA axis; how to order the health panels we will be discussing throughout the course.

2. **Gut health.** How leaky gut, bacteria, food sensitivities, diet, imbalanced bacteria affect methyla-

157

tion; how to understand your results; how to get rid of blocks to methylation.

3. **Adrenal health.** Why adrenal health is important to methylation; what your adrenal results could mean; how adrenal and oxidative stress can block methylation; how to get rid of the inhibitors to methylation.

4. **Blood work.** How to understand your thyroid levels, nutrients and homocysteine. What high and low homocysteine levels mean; symptoms of abnormal homocysteine levels; knowing what does to take; addressing hormones and methylation at your individual level.

5. **MTHFR and Genetic health.** Examining your genetic health report; how to check if you have high sulfur or nitric oxide; how other genes interplay with MTHFR; understanding the "downstream pathways" of methylation; when you should and should NOT take folate.

6. **Summary.** Maintenance and Stress Resilience, where to go from here; how to monitor your health over time; Q&A.

Visit DoctorDoni.com under "courses" to sign up for the Stress Warrior Course.

## Should I Do This Course Instead Of Seeing a Doctor?

This course is not intended to replace any medical treatment or support you may already be receiving. Rather, it will help you understand your condition more deeply, and learn how to take a **pro-active approach** to getting better. This course also offers **an economical alternative** for those who cannot afford to work one-on-one with a naturopathic doctor.

## How Much Does This Course Cost?

**This 6-part course costs $497.** This gives you access to the **sessions and recordings**, as well as to a special **Facebook group for support.** You will also have free access to a **pre-recorded introductory video seminar taught** by Dr. Doni called "MTHFR and Genetics" (normally $47) and Dr. Doni's Stress Remedy Leaky Gut Healing guide, meal plan, and email tips (value $97).

Sign up here.

## Are TheHealth Panels Included?

The costs of the panels are NOT included, as some people may have already done them.

While getting these health panels done is not mandatory, doing so can help you get the most out of the information Dr. Doni will be teaching you. If you wish to order the tests, you can choose them as optional "add-ons" when you purchase the course, or even after the course has begun.

**To reserve your spot in the class, be sure to sign up now.**

# Dr. Doni's 21-Day Stress Remedy Program

### What is Dr. Doni's Stress Remedy Program?

Dr. Doni's Stress Remedy Program is a self-guided 21-day program, specially designed to support you to:

- Implement CARE: Clean Eating, Adequate Sleep, Reduce Stress and Exercise regularly
- Start healing leaky gut
- Reduce inflammation throughout your entire body
- Restore optimal cortisol levels and healthy adrenal stress response
- Reduce exposure to toxins and pesticides
- Stabilize blood sugar levels
- It can also:
- Aid in weight loss
- Help balance hormones

- Help improve sleep
- Be an effective overall detoxification program
- Help "reset" your body when you've been feeling unwell for a long time.

## What symptoms can the Stress Remedy Program help alleviate?

The symptoms of leaky gut vary from person to person. The Stress Remedy Program can help alleviate many of the most common symptoms, such as:

- Chronic or frequent fatigue
- Chronic pain – muscle aches, frequent headaches, joint pain, etc.
- Sleep problems – inability to fall or stay asleep at night
- Digestive issues – bloating, reflux, IBS, discomfort
- Weight gain and difficulty losing weight
- Blood sugar imbalances
- Hormone imbalances
- Frequent skin rashes or allergic reactions
- Chronic infections – lungs, bladder, skin, sinus, vaginal, etc.
- Mood swings, anxiety, brain fog, etc.

# What's included in the program?

Dr. Doni's Stress Remedy Program consists of:

- Guidebook with 51 gluten-free, dairy-free recipes and meal plan
- Daily email tips to help guide you during the program
- Access to a private Facebook group, so you can interact with others on the program

**Optionally, you may purchase the following products to go with the program:**

- Pea Protein Shake:

https://www.drdonistore.com/Dr-Donis-Pea-Protein-Shake_p_733.html

- Leaky Gut Support:

https://www.drdonistore.com/Dr-Donis-Leaky-Gut-Support-61-oz_p_681.html

- Enzyme Support:

https://www.drdonistore.com/-Dr-Donis-Enzyme-Support-90-capsules_p_977.html

- Probiotic Support:

https://www.drdonistore.com/Dr-Donis-Probiotic-Support-60-vegetarian-capsules_p_271.html

# How much does it cost?

The price for the complete Stress Remedy Program is $97.

## Is this the right program for me?

The Stress Remedy Program is most suitable for people who:

- Have leaky gut OR suspect they might have it
- Want support to change their diet and implement self care strategies
- Want to try out a clean eating program to see if it helps alleviate their symptoms
- Feel confident about doing a health optimizing program on their own
- May not be ready to work one-to-one with a naturopathic doctor

Read all about the Stress Remedy Program, and sign up, here.

# What if I want more help?

**F**or those who desire a more personalized and comprehensive approach, Dr. Doni also offers a comprehensive one-on-one health consultation packages including a Adrenal Recovery and Wellness Package and Leaky Gut & Digestive Solutions Package. These consultation packages include recommended health panels, consultations with Dr. Doni, a private Facebook group and discounts on supplements.

## Adrenal Recovery and Wellness Package With Dr. Doni

**Dr. Doni's Adrenal Recovery and Wellness Package** is for you if you are suffering from one or more symptoms related to adrenal distress and cortisol imbalance (see below). This program is designed not only to help you recover from adrenal distress, but to STAY healthier and more resilient in the long term.

**Dr. Doni has been helping people recover from adrenal issues for over 18 years.** She's developed a proven system to specifically address the effects of stress, including leaky gut, hormone and neurotransmitter imbalances, as well as immune system issues and infections. She has written several books on the topic of stress recovery and trains practitioners to implement her approach. Dr. Doni knows what works and will show you exactly what to do.

## What are the adrenal glands?

The adrenal glands are endocrine glands about two inches in length that sit just above the kidneys. These glands produce our main stress hormones, **cortisol and adrenaline**, along with other hormones. Cortisol and adrenaline play crucial roles in your metabolism, sleep patterns, mood, energy, immunity, and overall wellness. That's because they are your body's main "stress responders" and are triggered whenever you experience *any* kind of stress, whether physical (illness, infection, injury, allergens, toxins, etc.) or emotional.

## What is "adrenal distress"?

Adrenal distress is a condition that arises when your body is exposed to more stress than it can handle and your cortisol and/or adrenaline levels become imbalanced. Trying to handle the stress, your adrenals can get stuck in "stress mode" and produce **too much OR too little** cortisol and adrenaline, or produce them at the **wrong time of day or night.** The longer your adrenals stay in "stress mode", the

more symptoms you are likely to develop, and the more difficult it can be to recover without guidance from a health professional.

## What are the symptoms of adrenal distress?

Adrenal distress is often responsible for a range of negative health symptoms, including:

- Poor sleep; waking unrested
- Exhaustion; needing naps during the day
- Frequent colds and flu
- Memory loss; brain fog
- Painful joints; frequent injuries
- Migraines and headaches
- Dizziness; weakness
- Blood sugar fluctuations
- Mood issues; depression; anxiety
- Allergies; autoimmunity; cancer
- Digestive issues
- Skin issues, such as eczema, psoriasis, hives, etc.
- Menstrual and fertility issues, such as PCOS, PMS, PMDD, peri-menopausal symptoms
- Cervical dysplasia, Lyme, Epstein Barr, and other chronic infections

- Autoimmunity, neurodegeneration, dementia, diabetes, and heart disease
- Unexplained weight loss or gain

When your adrenals are several impaired, you are more likely to experience more than one of these symptoms. Because these symptoms often *seem* to be unrelated, people may not suspect they are arising from the same root cause.

## Is this the same as "adrenal fatigue" or "adrenal burnout"?

**Yes and no.** These days, "adrenal fatigue" or "adrenal burnout" have become catch-all phrases to describe any kind of adrenal problem. But these terms can be misleading, as they *imply* your adrenals are under-producing cortisol and/or adrenaline. Adrenal problems can also arise when your body produces *too much* of these substances. For this reason, Dr. Doni prefers to use the terms "adrenal imbalance" or "adrenal distress".

## Why hasn't my doctor suggested I might have an adrenal problem?

Although scientists have been researching and writing papers on adrenal health for the past century, surprisingly few doctors ever mention "adrenals" to their patients or suggest that their symptoms might be adrenal-related. Instead, they tend to prescribe medications for the various symptoms. While these medications may stop the symptoms temporarily, **they don't address the underlying cause** and **can sometimes increase the severity** of the adrenal imbalance.

The doctors who *do* check your cortisol levels may only test them in the morning (when we know cortisol levels should vary throughout the day). While this kind of test might help identify the severe conditions such as Addison's disease or Cushing Syndrome (when your adrenals are severely under- or over-producing cortisol), **it is insufficient for patients whose adrenals are still functioning but not performing as they should.**

## What makes Dr. Doni's approach different?

**Good adrenal health depends on having a normal "adrenal curve",** where your cortisol levels are highest in the morning when you wake up, and gradually decrease throughout the day until they are lowest at night when you want to go to sleep. To obtain an accurate picture of your adrenal curve, **Dr. Doni checks your cortisol four times within a single day** (morning, midday, evening, and bedtime). This is done with either a saliva or urine collection. She also checks your adrenaline levels.

Dr. Doni knows that **cortisol affects our digestive, immune, endocrine (hormones),** and **nervous systems** and finds that it is essential to address these systems for a full adrenal recovery.

To get a clear picture of stress has affected these systems, Dr. Doni will ask you do a food sensitivities panel (to identify possible digestive issues, such as **leaky gut**), blood work (to identify **blood sugar, hemoglobin, immune system, hormones, thyroid**, etc.), and a urine panel to measure your levels of **adrenaline** and **neurotransmitters** (to see what is going on in your nervous system).

Once you have a clear picture of what is going on in your body, Dr. Doni will work closely with you to address your adrenal issues through **diet, nutrients, herbs,** and **lifestyle changes**, so your body can heal itself – naturally and without medications. Because good adrenal function is so integral to your overall wellness, you will start to **feel healthier and more resilient to stress in the future.**

## Why is a "package" better than "a la carte"?

There are several advantages to choosing one of Dr. Doni's consultation packages:

- All treatment packages **cost significantly less** than the same services "a la carte".

- You will be entitled to a **10% discount on ANY supplements** purchased from **DrDoniStore.com** for the duration of your package.

- You will have access to a **private Facebook group**, where you can **ask questions (and get answers!)** about your health issue(s), share experiences with other patients, and take advantage of **special "members only" discounts on health supplements** (for the duration of your package).

- You will receive a free paperback copy of Dr. Doni's book *The Stress Remedy* (value $25).

- You will receive the Stress Remedy Program daily **health tips** by email for 21 days, including the **21-day meal plan and recipes.** (value $97)

- Best of all, patients who commit to a 6-month package **tend to *stick* to their health regimen more faithfully**, thus increasing their chances for better results.

## What is included in this package?

### HEALTH PANELS

In this package, the following panels are included*:

- 4-timed salivary or urinary cortisol panel

- Urinary neurotransmitter panel (serotonin, GABA, adrenaline, etc.)

- IgG and IgA food sensitivities panel for 96 foods

Some additional blood work may also be required (example: metabolic panel, thyroid, etc.), which can be done either through your doctor or through Dr. Doni's office.

\* *If you have recently done this panel, ask your doctor to send the results to Dr. Doni's office, and the price of your package will be adjusted accordingly.*

# CONSULTATIONS (7)

You will have SEVEN private consultations with Dr. Doni, spread out over a 6-month period.

These include:

- ONE comprehensive 60-minute consultation to discuss your health issues and individualize your plan.
- ONE extended 45-minute consultation to go through the results of your health panels and give recommendations.
- THREE regular 30-minute consultations to assess progress, adjust regimen and address any other issues.
- TWO brief 15-minute consultations to create an ongoing maintenance plan and discuss any other issues.

Patients are responsible for scheduling all consultations and follow-ups either via email

(schedule@doctordoni.com) or online at

https://doctordoni.com/schedule.

We recommend scheduling well in advance to ensure availability at your preferred time.

KINDLY NOTE: All consultations must be completed within the agreed 6-month package timeframe.

Additional consultations may be added as needed.

# SUPPLEMENTS and NUTRIENTS

While this package does not include supplements, it entitles you to a 10% discount on ANY supplements you purchase from **DrDoniStore.com** during your six months of work together.

# ADDITIONAL SUPPORT

You will have access to a **private Facebook group**, where you can **ask questions (and get answers!)** about your health issues and treatment program, **share experiences** with other patients, and take advantage of **special offers** on health supplements, available only to members of the group.

# EXTRAS INCLUDED

As part of your package, you will also receive:

- A summarized list of foods for you to avoid, based on your results

- A paperback copy of Dr. Doni's book *The Stress Remedy* (retail value $25)

- Three weeks' worth of daily "Stress Remedy" health tips (via email) to support you with any diet and health changes you make during your program (retail value $97)

## Do I need to come to your office?

It is optional to meet in person in one of Dr. Doni's offices. Dr. Doni ls also available to meet "virtually" (on phone or video call), especially if they live far away.

## How much does this package cost?

**The total cost of this 6-month package is $2,697.** You may opt to pay in two installments: $1,700 upon your first visit, and the balance of $997 one month later.

THIS PACKAGE gives you $305 in savings over "a la carte" pricing for the same services,

PLUS 10% off ALL your supplements for six months, and access to the private Facebook group.

**NOTE:** *Much of the initial fee covers the cost of the IgG and IgA food sensitivities panel. If you have recently taken a food sensitivities test, ask your doctor to send the results to Dr. Doni's office, and the price of your package will be reduced accordingly.*

## How do I get started?

Simply apply to work with Dr. Doni by sending an email to schedule@doctordoni.com, or by submitting your request at https://doctordoni.com/schedule.

# About Dr. Doni Wilson, Naturopathic Doctor

DR. DONI WILSON, N.D. is a Doctor of Naturopathic Medicine, natural health expert, nutritionist and midwife. She specializes in gluten sensitivity, intestinal permeability, adrenal stress, insulin resistance, neurotransmitter imbalances, hypothyroidism, women's health issues, autoimmunity and genetic variations called "SNPs," which can have a profound impact upon your health.

For nearly 20 years, she has helped women, men and children overcome their most perplexing health challenges and achieve their wellness goals by crafting individualized strategies that address the whole body and the underlying causes of health issues.

DR. DONI is the creator of The Stress Remedy Programs and author of The Stress Remedy: Master Your Body's Synergy & Optimize Your Health as well as the #1 bestselling books Stress Remedies: How to Reduce Stress and Boost Your Health in Just 15 Minutes a Day, The Natural Insomnia Solution, and Stress Warrior.

Professional affiliations...

- American Association of Naturopathic Physicians (past board member)
- New York Association of Naturopathic Physicians (president and executive director 2003 – 2013)
- American Association of Naturopathic Midwives (past board member)
- Connecticut Naturopathic Physicians Association
- Endocrinology Association of Naturopathic Physicians
- Pediatric Association of Naturopathic Physicians
- Association for the Advancement of Restorative Medicine

# Book Description

Reverse engineer your health and get your energy, focus, mood and optimal weight back by following this three-step approach to becoming a warrior to stress. Stress is a part of life. I can show you how to become resilient to stress so it doesn't wreck your business and your life.